Smart & Caring

SMART & CARING

A Donor's Guide to Major Gifting

Richard & Linda Livingston

with contributions by
Kathleen Hammond, *Attorney at Law*
William Rogers, C.P.A.

PUBLISHING • *Louisville, Colorado*

Published by
RDL PUBLISHING
Website: **www.smartandcaring.com**

Editing: Lynn Arts
Book design, composition, and production management:
    Polly Christensen

International Standard Book Number: ISBN 0-9674130-0-1
Library of Congress Number: 99-093522

This book has been printed on acid-free recycled paper
using soy ink.

Printed in the United States of America by
Johnson Publishing • Boulder, Colorado

10 9 8 7 6 5 4 3 2 1

Contents

Tables & Figures

To the caregivers

Acknowledgments

To the many who reviewed, encouraged, assisted, insisted and suggested, our deepest thanks.

To name a few: Josie Heath, Jo Arnold, John Neville, Connie Friehauf, Marie Wheatly, John Dreves, Bob Perry, Judi Shaffer, Brad Shaffer, David Miller, Howard Teague, Clair Beckmann, Sharon Svendsen, Brad Bickham, Sue and Dave French, Kathy Coyne, Yvonne Williams, Mary Hey, Peter Arts, Jennifer McKeown, and Jon Hamill,

And a special, special thanks to the donors who read our early drafts, and met with us to critique and encourage. You know who you are, and to us, you are very special.

And to our professional partners: Kathleen Hammond, Bill Rogers, Lynn Arts, and Polly Christensen; we thank you.

Foreword

DICK AND LINDA LIVINGSTON have been my clients for many years. When we first met, the Livingstons were comfortable—day-to-day needs could be satisfied without too much difficulty. But they knew that they would inherit some day and could see the need to restructure their estate plan to acknowledge this reality.

As a result of this estate planning effort and other influences in their lives over the next few years, they took the step into stewardship mode. They came to be less interested in increasing or even maintaining their net worth and more interested in creating sound ways to share their financial good fortune with others.

The Livingstons made the decision to move into "stewardship" thoughtfully, patiently, and methodically. In the process of reaching their decision, a lot of questions arose. Because of the way the Livingstons use their resources (which include their advisors), Bill Rogers and I were able to participate in, or at least be cognizant of, those questions and the processes through which the Livingstons answered them. As the process developed, we urged Dick and Linda to share their experiences by writing this book. We believe they can serve as guides and role models for others who might be in a position to make charitable gifting an important part of their lives.

As a trust and estate attorney, I bring the traditional lawyer's view to this effort. The traditional attorney's role is to determine and create the devices—the tools—to accomplish the client's objectives. The question is "Which tool is the right one for this individual, this family, this circumstance?" The answer that comes to mind for most attorneys is "The one that saves the most tax dollars." That answer is based on our training, and it is reinforced by the avalanche of technical professional articles that cross our desks. It also assumes that saving tax dollars is the client's objective—indeed, the client's top priority.

Any estate-planning device has many ramifications, one of which is likely to be saving taxes. When tax planning is the highest priority, all other objectives must be subordinate, even if they may be affected adversely. In my experience, this process has resulted in the creation of some very effective tax-savings devices—and a few very unhappy clients. This has been the case even when the client seemed totally on board with the goal of minimizing tax dollars.

Although everyone involved in the process was talking tax savings, those clients had certain unidentified values they were not really willing to sacrifice in order to reduce taxes. There have been circumstances where I knew intuitively that a client had some level of discomfort (perhaps deeply buried) with my proposed tax-savings strategy. Nonetheless, I could not get to what that client *really* wanted without going through a process that I could not define and that seemed outside my traditional role.

Then the Livingstons became clients. As I worked with Dick and Linda, the process gradually became clear. It meant stepping beyond the assumption that tax savings were the prime objective and therefore must define the context for creating the overall plan. Instead, I observed Dick and Linda working out a hierarchy of objectives, priorities, and values against which any tool and its implications would be tested. Saving taxes was definitely on the list; it just wasn't at the top.

The process took some time, but eventually we were able to articulate a hierarchy of values with respect to their estate planning. I believe we now know how to ask the kinds of questions of one another that set the context for decisions that need to be made.

Now, when I meet new clients, I ask them to discuss the context in which their estate-planning decisions are to be made, and I listen. Often it becomes clear that there is no definable context. At that point the question is whether to impose the classic tax-savings focus or to suggest that perhaps they could develop a context that is more individualized and satisfying by first identifying their values. I've learned to take the time to discover how important objectives other than tax savings may be to the client.

Becoming involved in the process of defining client values suggests a broader role for many of us as attorneys—one that promises great rewards to everyone on both sides of the attorney's desk. I offer Dick and Linda's own words, which I believe will be illuminating to attorneys (and other professional advisors), as well as inspiring to people seeking counselors to whom they can relate: "We as clients come to the lawyer's table awed, innocent, and overpowered. By establishing an atmosphere where clients realize that their job (and opportunity) is to establish what they want their wealth to accomplish, the result of the process is likely to be much more rewarding for the client and attorney alike."

—*Kathleen Hammond*

Introduction

Who Are We?

Dick and Linda Livingston

We are your typical friends and neighbors. We are in our mid 60s, retired, with lots of grandchildren. Average, perhaps, with three exceptions. First, in 1993, we lost a daughter to cancer, a loss that has made us much more sensitive to those in need. That experience became a catalyst for our pursuing a serious gifting program. Second, we found ourselves with a substantial net worth at this stage of our lives, and third, we have a strong tendency to analyze choices.

Kathleen Hammond

Kathleen is a trust and estate attorney who is a partner in a major Boulder law firm. She is our attorney and our friend. Kathleen brings a wide range of experience to this effort, both as an attorney and as a person who knows and understands people and family relationships.

Where legal matters are stated as fact in this book, Kathleen has worked to ensure that our narrative is technically correct. Where we have commented on legal matters (and lawyers) as opinion, Kathleen may or may not agree with our observations. We take full responsibility for our comments and opinions.

Bill Rogers

Bill is a certified public accountant (CPA) with a Denver accounting firm. He has extensive experience in complex tax matters as they affect family-related estates and trusts. In addition to serving as a professional advisor to us, Bill is our friend.

Bill's input has been invaluable in giving direction to the family financial programming effort. Although Bill has been the brains behind the tax calculations that are the backbone of our family financial computer program—and although he has labored to check the work on the entire program—the responsibility for its accuracy must remain with us.

How Did We Come to Write This Book?

As we went through the process that led us to become major donors, what we searched for most and found least was a *comprehensive* view of the world of personal gifting. We searched for a source that included all the pieces: family gifting, charitable gifting, family issues, personal values, tools and techniques for giving, how to interact with professionals, and so on. We did not find it. We found that each component was generally viewed independently of the others. So this effort turned out to be a gathering and developing of thoughts, concepts, and techniques that work for us.

This is not a do-it-yourself book on how to do your own legal and accounting work. In fact, everything we have learned has convinced us that doing your own legal or accounting work is very unwise. The IRS recognizes quite a number of tax-efficient ways to gift money, and the rules are fairly clear. However, the IRS is quite unforgiving if you don't follow those rules to the letter. In addition, the rules are continually changing. We recommend that you see *your* lawyer and accountant; you'll be glad you did.

Will This Book Be of Interest to You?

If you meet the following criteria, this book may be just what you are looking for:

- ❧ You have financial resources to spare.
- ❧ You like the concept of sharing with others.
- ❧ You don't mind considering your own mortality.
- ❧ You want your giving to be done in a tax-efficient manner.

Major Gifting: A Definition

As we started our research into the world of nonprofits and major gifting, we had no idea what was generally viewed as a "major gift." Those words made us think of a public figure donating a million dollars or more to a university, a medical research program, or some other worthy institution. Although we were in a position to do more than we had in the past, we were not in that category.

As time went on, we learned that the bar for being considered a major donor is much lower than we had thought. Most charities do not get the bulk of their money from large "windfall" donations. Rather their income typically comes from many, many smaller gifts, plus a few good-sized, but not overwhelming, major gifts.

From a charity's point of view, the perception as to whether a gift is "major" is no doubt closely related to the percentage of their total budget that gift represents. A small local church may consider $1,000 to be big bucks; to a big university, hospital complex, or national health-related nonprofit, $10,000 may be viewed as welcome, but not overwhelming at all. Very subjective stuff here.

Subjective or not, we have come to think of "major gifting" as being in the ranges we are about to describe. As you read the book, remember that we are thinking in these terms. For an individual gift to a charity, $1,000 to $2,000 might be thought of as the entry level for "major gifting." As you move into the $5,000 to $10,000 range, you are certainly in major gifting territory. Of course, there is no cap on these ranges.

For total annual gifting by an individual or family, we think of $3,000 to $5,000 as the entry level for being considered major donors. As you move up into the $15,000 to $30,000 per year range, you have certainly become very welcome major donors. No cap here, either.

If you want a firsthand reading of how much people really give to individual organizations, look at the donor list that often accompanies the annual report of a charity or peruse the donor plaques in their lobbies. You won't find too many people up there in the top tiers.

Objectives, Hopes, and Dreams

You might wonder why a very private couple, retiring by nature and quite uncomfortable being in the limelight, would choose to write a book that says quite a lot about their personal situation and outlook. Quite simply, many of the professionals and donors that we have worked with have told us we take a unique approach to major gifting and have encouraged us to share our thinking with others. They have urged us to record our experiences, conclusions, and actions in this very personal process. To the extent that what we have learned may serve as a catalyst for and guide to others interested in pursuing gifting, we are pleased to do so.

Our fondest hope is that, with this book, we can help to increase the size of the total "gifting pie." We hope that over the next few years, an increasing amount of private assets will move to the multitude of good causes, large and small, that can make use of these major donations. We would like to feel that our shared experiences might influence even a few more people to benefit from the extraordinary rewards of becoming more deeply involved with the nonprofit community.

How the Book Is Organized

We believe there are three distinct sides to the major gifting story: the personal, the technical, and the financial. These pieces are not only quite distinct, but the time-frame for a donor's interest is also likely to vary from person to person. Thus, we have considered each of the three sections independently, so that they can be read and used at whatever time works for you. The fourth section of the book provides a summary of the process and what we have learned.

Section 1. The Personal Side

The first section deals with the people and personal issues of major gifting. It addresses family issues, relationships with advisors, selecting charities, the rewards of gifting, and the personal side of working through the major gifting process.

Section 2. The Technical Side

The second section addresses tax issues and the tools and techniques of major gifting. It gives a layman's overview of the tax-advantaged methods of gifting, set forth in an organized, structured, and quantified way.

Section 3. The Financial Side

The third section offers a comprehensive overview of the numbers of major gifting. It includes summary graphs and tables showing the impact of various lifetime gifting options on taxes and net worth. We have made the spreadsheet templates that generate these calculations available for downloading from the Internet.

Section 4. The Summary

This final section provides a comprehensive summary of what we have learned as we have worked through the process.

THE
PERSONAL
SIDE

1
The Process Begins

IN 1994, OUR NET WORTH was about to be substantially increased by an inheritance. Thus began our education in the world of complex estate settlement and our preparation for the interesting world of major gifting. We soon found ourselves with much more than we needed to live on, and we pondered what to do with the extra money.

Taking the broadest view of our options, we realized that we, like everyone else, had two choices: We could (1) spend it, or (2) give it away. And within that general framework, we concluded that again, like everyone else, we had three choices as to whom we might give the portion of our net worth that we did not spend. We could:

* Give to family and friends
* Give to charities
* Give to government

Whatever we don't spend, we will give! No other options. This realization may sound trivial, but it wasn't. It led to everything that followed.

Implementing the "spend some" strategy was easy. We take higher-class tours, redecorate the house more often, and buy better computer toys. But beyond that, not too much has changed in our personal spending habits.

"Give to family" has been a lot tougher to implement. The core issue was and is how to do the most good, while doing the least damage. Working this out has not been an easy task at all. The second strategy, "give to charity," and the related third "give to government" are the focus of much of what follows in this book.

At the beginning of our odyssey toward becoming major donors, we were rather detached citizens of our community, duty-driven to give modest amounts of time and money to charity, but hardly major participants. We were quite naive about the world of lawyers, accountants, financial advisors, development directors, and so on. Tax law was a fog, as was pretty much anything to do with investing and estate planning. (We will mention estate planning now and again, but only where it is relevant to the issues of gifting. Estate planning has been well covered in other publications.)

We found it liberating when we realized that we had already decided to become major givers. The only questions to be resolved were who the recipients would be, how much we would give, when we would give, and what gifting techniques we would use. Our journey has now brought us to the point where we have become major financial donors, quite deeply involved in the nonprofit community. In the process, we have gone from having a moderately organized view of our net worth, both current and projected, to a very structured view.

When it came to taxation, we eventually learned that through our gifting choices, we could have a great influence on how much we "gave" to the government.

We have observed that people with a substantial net worth often fall into the trap of worrying that they won't have enough money, and they just become increasingly frugal—and that much richer—as they get older. In many cases we have seen this focus on retention and even growth of wealth become central to people's lives, in effect denying them the opportunity to enjoy the wealth they have been fortunate enough to acquire. We did not want this to be our pattern.

The process of working this all out has been interesting, and the results have been incredibly rewarding. Stay with us, and we'll tell you all about it.

2
Personal Issues

MAJOR GIFTING IS BOTH a personal and a financial matter. It is often difficult to keep the two in balance. The personal (soft) issues may fade into the background, while the more measurable financial (hard) issues become the more influential factors. In fact, the subject of major gifting is often approached as strictly a financial matter—as an issue of tax implications, sort of a game with the IRS to find the cleverest approach for saving on taxes.

We think that taxes and the other mechanical issues related to major gifting certainly have their place, but for us, the core of a really rewarding gifting program lies in creating a balance. We think donors need to be smart in their choice of gifting methods but also caring in their approach toward issues that are important to them as individuals. The two can work well together.

Once we concluded that, yes, we were going to become major donors, it became clear that we had quite a number of things to think through. Saying that we were going to give and actually doing so turned out to be two very different things. As with almost everyone else, our financial life had been focused on earning, saving, and spending. Actually giving—now that was something else. As we look back on the process, it is easy to see what issues we were working through, but it was not at all clear at the time. We now know that we were confronting obstacles to giving, reasons for giving, and our basic value system.

This chapter discusses the soft issues of giving: basic motivation, family issues, and personal values. The next chapter will treat the all-important family gifting issues in more depth.

Reasons for Giving

We have been asked why we give, and we haven't been able to answer that question very well. On the surface, our decision was intuitive. It was just there. We never gave much thought as to *whether* to give; we moved right on to the questions of *how* to give, how much to give, and to whom to give.

As we think about it now, we see that two key levels of motivation were working here. First, there was this basic feeling of "it's the right thing to do," that feeling from back in our upbringing and our life experiences that told us it would be good to do this. Our reasons to give certainly built on what have become our basic values—our very personal sense of "the right thing to do."

On a more pragmatic level, we think there were also a number of specific issues that moved us from thinking about giving to actually giving. These were the consideration of some very specific *reasons to give* and perhaps even more important, the need to deal with some serious *obstacles to giving*.

Perhaps it takes all three—(1) an underlying *inclination to give*, (2) a review of your *reasons to give*, and (3) the working out of *obstacles to giving*—to produce a real live "major donor."

First, let's examine some generic reasons for giving. The list that follows includes some of the reasons we think people give, along with how we rate these motivations as part of our own giving:

* **To "give back."** We have needed help ourselves at times, and we have gotten it. Giving provides a sense of payback for us.

* **To support hands-on caregivers.** We greatly admire those who actively provide help to those who need it. We want to do what we can to support them in their extraordinary work.

* **As a living memorial to a family member.** This was certainly a factor for us.

* **Because it seems a better use of the money than handing it over for taxes.** We think well-run private charities do a much more efficient job of routing money to those in need than the government does.

* **To meet a group of people we admire.** Giving introduces us to a community of people we thoroughly enjoy being part of.

* **In response to a fund-raiser who asks for a donation.** Statistics seem to show that much of the motivation for giving comes from the initiative of a fund-raiser asking for a donation. That may be, but it has not been the case for us.

* **To make fundamental changes in society.** This is a real motivator for many major donors.

* **Out of religious motivation.** Statistics show that a very large percentage of charitable gifting can be identified as growing out of the donor's religious convictions.

* **To ease a sense of guilt.** We suppose everyone has some degree of guilt about being financially comfortable, if only buried deep down inside. Are we motivated by some sense of unease over having plenty when others do not? We don't think guilt is a major factor behind our giving. We haven't pondered over that aspect very much.

* **To secure a tax deduction (to save money).** In the

sense that the more we save, the more we can give, yes, this is a motivator for giving. But we do not view giving as a tool for increasing our net worth or our income.

- **To continue a family tradition.** Not really; neither side of our families was deeply involved in the charitable community.

- **To win public or private recognition.** We are not at all interested in public recognition for our giving, but private recognition has probably been a factor.

As you weigh these reasons for giving, you may well find that each has a very different priority for you.

Obstacles to Giving

Next we look at a generic list of obstacles to giving that most people probably need to work through. Once again we have provided some observations on how we dealt with them. Most certainly your priority of concern and your resolution of each obstacle will be different than ours.

- **Concern about running out of money.** We didn't really have deep concerns about running out of money. We were sure that we could gift more than we had in the past without getting into financial trouble; we just didn't know how much we could afford. Could we give away $5,000, or $20,000, or maybe even $50,000 a year? We really didn't know. We needed to get a handle on this quantification issue before we could become serious donors.

- **Marginal knowledge of the nonprofit world.** We knew little about what was out there. We did not have a network. We really didn't know where to start.

- **Concern about selecting the right nonprofits.** Like most people these days, we were quite aware of well-publicized abuses in the nonprofit community. We wanted no part of giving money to organizations that were likely to misuse it.

- **Would it be preferable to spend the money rather than give it away?** Sure, upgrading our lifestyle was appealing, but we had no desire for a major change. We felt we could spend more on ourselves and still be major donors.

- **Taking pleasure in watching the net worth grow.** It was great to see the extra money in the bank, to watch it start to grow. Once we came to understand that most of this growth would be lost to taxes, the "fun" diminished rapidly.

- **Lack of time to investigate major gifting.** It looked like it would take a lot of time to do this major gifting job right. Even though we were retired, we were busy. We simply decided that this was a priority. Somewhat to our surprise, we found that rather than being a chore, the investigative process was a rewarding experience.

- **Unresolved plans for leaving the estate to family.** Coming up with a plan for gifting and leaving money to family took a great deal of thought and effort. However, we knew that this was something that had to be done as part of our estate planning, no matter what we decided about other giving.

- **Reluctance to sell principal.** We have long been at ease with the concept of selling or giving principal, but we do know that this can be a great obstacle for many.

- ❦ **Plain old inertia.** Inertia was not much of a problem for us; we had already determined that becoming major donors was a priority in our lives.

- ❦ **Lack of an appropriate lawyer or accountant.** Since we had established good relationships with a lawyer and an accountant as we went through the process of creating our estate plan, we were in good shape in this department as we moved into planning for major gifting.

- ❦ **Aversion to paying professional fees.** We had rationalized that paying the cost of professional advice was part of the gifting process.

- ❦ **Consensus between spouses.** We tend to forget that the issue of consensus between spouses can be a real problem for many. We're lucky here; we share common values, and we usually agree on these things.

- ❦ **People would find out.** In the beginning, privacy issues were a real concern to us. We didn't want everyone to know we had money to give away. We have become much less concerned about this over time.

As you can see, we were most concerned about (1) not having an adequate understanding of our long-term net worth; (2) unresolved family-gifting issues; and (3) our lack of knowledge about the nonprofit community. So, these were the obstacles that we tackled.

We realize that any obstacle can turn out to be the "fatal flaw" that might stand in the way of doing major gifting. Very few of them are easy to deal with. Our suggestion? Take them on, one by one—deal with each in turn. If you don't work them all through, it will be hard to sustain a gifting program over the years.

Personal Values

As we worked through our motivations and concerns, it became clear to us that the foundation for our decisions and actions lay in our sense of personal values. As Kathleen pointed out in the Foreword, our collective experience taught us all how central personal values are in developing an appropriate estate and gifting plan. We have become convinced that understanding our personal values was the key to creating an estate and gifting plan that we will be comfortable with for the long term.

You will find some overlap between our list of personal values with the reasons for giving that we offered earlier. That's because many of our values and priorities translate directly into reasons for giving.

- **Personal comfort and security.** It was very important to us to know that we were not going to run out of money, and that we would be able to retain our chosen lifestyle.

- **Family relationships and dynamics.** We prize family relationships above all. This feeling was certainly strengthened by the loss of a daughter, but it has always been central for us.

- **Gifting to family.** Sharing our assets and giving in a way that helps rather than hurts is high on our priority list.

- **Gifting for charitable purposes.** This has also become a high priority for us.

- **Simplicity and economy of administration, plus the avoidance of intrusive complexity.** We like to go forward. We like to "do it once and do it right." We are interested in managing our affairs as necessary, but it is not a hobby of ours. We don't like to be controlled by money—we like to control it. Sorting through legal, accounting, and tax-related documents is not enjoyable to us. We like to keep the financial side as simple as possible so that we can invest our time in more rewarding activities.

* **Tax savings.** We are certainly interested in tax savings, largely because the more we save, the more we can give to the charities of our choice.

* **Give to charities rather than to government.** We also feel strongly that well-run charities will do a better job administering the assets we give than the government agencies that would otherwise receive our money.

* **Preserving wealth so that it benefits as many future generations as possible.** We do not feel a strong need to set up a dynasty. We like the idea that our children and grandchildren will have the benefits and freedoms that come from some financial independence, as we have had, but establishing a high level of wealth for future generations is not a driving force for us.

* **Protecting family members who are improvident or unprepared.** This is certainly a factor for us, especially as we look at our grandchildren's generation. We do worry that we may inadvertently do damage to upcoming generations by leaving them money.

* **Retaining control of the estate.** Having "control" of one sort or another is important to everyone, ourselves included. But in our case, having direct control over the money is not as important as having control over how we spend our time.

* **Gaining recognition for contributions to charitable causes.** The knowledge that the assets we donate are well-used is the only form of "recognition" that we seek. For us, public recognition is a minus, not a plus.

* **Desire to change society.** This is a powerful motivator for many. We never thought it was an important value for us, but here we are writing a book with the objective of encouraging a wider base of the population to do major gifting. Maybe we subscribe to this "change society" value more than we had realized.

What Is Your "Right Thing to Do?"

Many would say they give because "it's the right thing to do." We say that. (Have you ever heard anyone say they want to "do the *wrong* thing"?) But ask ten people how they feel about this, and once you get beyond motherhood and apple pie, you will probably get ten very different answers. So, what are *your* values? What is important to you? What do you want *your* money to accomplish? If you can arrive at well-thought-out answers to those questions, it will likely make the other decisions regarding major giving much easier.

3
Family Issues

Giving to Family: Risky Business

We think family gifting is the most difficult part of major gifting. Mistakes can certainly be made in charitable giving, but no real damage is likely to be done. In the case of family giving, however, real damage can be done. First there is the danger of doing harm to family relationships, and second, there is a chance that a gift might harm people (particularly young people) by diminishing their self-esteem and perhaps limiting their potential for healthy self-development. All of us have seen situations where things have come too easily for someone we know, particularly in that person's younger years, and their development as a self-reliant individual has been hindered.

Many of us have witnessed or heard of lasting family rifts that have developed over money—in particular over the inheritance of money or possessions. We suspect that it is a rare family that does not find itself, after the settlement of an estate, with some bruised feelings that take a long time to heal, if ever. The most dramatic cases make the headlines, but most of these family squabbles are probably known only to friends of the family members.

The Potential for Family Stress

Probably the primary means of gifting to family is to leave them money and personal property, with or without benefit of an estate plan. Another common approach is to set up some type of trust, which provides the donor with more control over how and when the funds become available. (Control from the grave, some would say.) Annual gifting is also common. All three methods leave plenty of room for family stresses and strains to develop.

As noted earlier, we recently went through an estate-settlement process that led to a substantial increase in our net worth. The process was long and painful. The complex legal structure that had been set in place—which may or may not have really saved much in the way of taxes—predetermined that settling would be an expensive, ponderous, and frustrating process. (By the way, if you are really mad at someone and want to punish him or her unmercifully, make them your executor or personal representative. That'll fix 'em!)

In time we did get through the whole process with family relationships intact. However, it was clear to us that for cases where family members have very different interests, the settlement process offers plenty of opportunity for stresses, strains, and outright conflict. Just because the process is so complicated and drags out for so long, there are a multitude of chances for misunderstanding and frustration.

The one and only redeeming value of this experience was how much we learned from it. We came to understand how important it was to be diligent in writing our estate plan to ensure that our descendants and executors would not be saddled with the same burdens. We learned to strive for cost-effective simplicity. We tried hard to avoid situations where our family members would have to "do business" among themselves or with a large number of advisors in order to resolve the estate. We also learned to be sensitive to ongoing family relationships when we made arrangements for charitable gifting.

Expectations for Our Future Family Relationships

We have high hopes that our family members will continue to have cordial relationships over time. Although the three family groups get along quite well, they are different in many ways. They live in different parts of the country and enjoy very different lifestyles. Their financial goals also differ, as do their plans for the future.

Given that the family relationships seem to be quite good, our challenge is to set up our estate plan and do our gifting in such a way that it doesn't interfere with these healthy relationships. We need to be sure that we don't plant the seeds of conflict for future generations. For us, the first rule of estate planning and family gifting is the same as the doctor's Hippocratic oath: "Do no harm."

Family Gifting Without Damage

We pondered, for some time, how best to give to family without doing damage. These are tough issues. One school of thought argues against giving anything to your children because it might destroy their initiative and sense of self-worth. (*The Millionaire Next Door,* by Thomas J. Stanley and William D. Danko, has an extensive chapter on gifting to family. They don't much like it.) Some people believe that everything should be put in trust, with outside control, to protect family members from themselves. Others feel that lots of money should be given to the next generation so that they can "have a better life" or "get a good start."

We think the truth lies somewhere in between these extremes. We found the decision to be very dependent on our children's ages, their existing self-motivation, and any number of other individual factors.

Our surviving children and their spouses are mature, having experienced many years of struggling on their own, "learning the value of money," so gifting to them is not a major concern. Providing for our daughter's son in a way that respects his right to make choices as he becomes a mature adult while protecting him from too much, too soon as a young man, was much more complicated, requiring some fairly involved trust work. We have our fingers crossed. We do have generalized concerns about our grandchildren. Who knows what kind of person a child will be at age 18, 21, or even 30? There are no easy, "one size fits all" answers to that one.

Resolving these issues and making a plan is an integral part of creating a strategy for major gifting.

Involving Family in Estate and Gifting Programs

Given all the above, we looked very cautiously at long-term family partnerships, and family foundations as tools for tax savings. Such partnerships do require family members to work with each other on money-related matters over the long haul. Not the best thing for every family, we would guess. We felt it was not right for our family; however, it might be just the thing for you. We urge you to give a lot of thought to these issues.

We tend to think it is unwise to force or even encourage family members into business relationships that they may or may not wish to be part of, no matter how good the tax savings might be. Again, this is largely an estate-planning issue, but it is certainly a factor in many of the more complex gifting arrangements.

Other Family Members' Views on Major Charitable Gifting

Major gifting can raise issues of fairness in some families. For example, a child might view major gifting to charities as cheating him or her out of a "rightful" inheritance. (Money doesn't necessarily bring out the best in people.) We don't anticipate this problem with our family members; at least, we haven't seen any signs of it. However, we do know that we need to be sensitive about such issues. We've found that the best way to deal with the subject is basic candor. We have chosen to share our long-term family financial plan and the related plans for major gifting with our family. There will be no dramatic surprises from the "reading of the will" in our family's future.

4
Advice and Advisors

OUR NATURAL TENDENCY, as we began the major gifting process, was to look to the experts to tell us what to do. Why should we have to reinvent the wheel? Couldn't we just go to the right book, magazine article, or professional advisor and find the answers? We certainly didn't find that to be the case.

Yes, the fund-raising community offers many publications, but those references generally take the fund-raiser's point of view, which may be somewhat at odds with the donor's point of view. We wound up gathering pieces of the whole from a wide range of sources, including lawyers, accountants, money managers, brokers, charities, books, and magazines. Our own experiences and good old common sense also played a large role in leading us to the insights we have reached.

The Professionals: An Overview

We have found that making effective use of professional assistance has a lot to do with your expectations. It was important to understand what the different types of professionals do and do not do. Are the following comments on experts and other information sources generalizations? Absolutely. Are all lawyers (or accountants, financial advisors, or fund-raisers) exactly alike? Certainly not. Then how can we, in good conscience, make the sweeping statements that we do? Quite simply because you have to start somewhere to establish reasonable expectations. It seems to us that using such generalizations, oversimplified though they may be, is a practical approach to the problem.

Lawyers

Lawyers provide you with the legal machinery to accomplish your objectives. It is not their responsibility to advise you on what your life objectives should be, and many lawyers are not going to be comfortable playing that role. Lawyers generally work on a fee-per-hour basis.

Accountants

Accountants provide you with appropriate financial tools and follow through to optimize tax benefits while minimizing tax problems connected with the financial actions you choose to take. It is not their responsibility, nor is it generally within their comfort zone to advise you on your life objectives. Accountants also work on a fee-per-hour basis.

Financial Advisors

This umbrella term covers a great deal of territory. Financial professionals range from the broker who may advise you on your investment choices and handle the mechanics of investment activities, all the way up to full-spectrum financial planners who may counsel you on your life objectives, in addition to offering you a variety of financial services to achieve those ends.

Payment methods range from commission on products sold to an hourly fee for service. The skill levels, training, and certification of these professionals can be all over the map. Their titles are equally diverse and may or may not be somewhat inflated.

Many in this field do feel that they have the responsibility and expertise to move beyond basic investment advice to counsel you on the broader aspects of your life objectives. We're sure that some financial advisors are qualified to do this—but others are not. You might not be comfortable re-

ceiving advice from someone who stands to collect a commission on the products that he or she sells to you; many
people feel more comfortable working with an advisor who
is directly compensated for the advice he or she provides.

We have found it helpful to remember that this is, after
all, a service industry. The key seems to rest in finding the organization (and the individual within that organization) that
is best qualified to supply the services you want and need.
(Hint: What services do *you* want and need?)

The Fund-Raisers

We have found that the people we have met who are involved
in fund-raising, by and large, are a great bunch of people.
They all may be helpful to you at one time or another.

Staff Members

Medium to large organizations generally have someone in
charge of fund-raising, often with the title "Development Director." Smaller organizations may include this function as
part of the role of the head of the organization, who often
has the title of "Executive Director." No matter what the title
is, you'll usually find someone whose job (mission, calling,
or whatever) is to get out the word and bring in the money.

We have found that these folks are most helpful with information about their organizations and related gifting techniques. That is their job, and in our experience, most of them
do it very well. We have also found that they are delighted to
tell you about what their organizations do, in as much detail
as you are willing to absorb. Do talk to them—this kind of contact is a large part of feeling good about giving. But please do
remember that although they may have some interesting

ideas on how best to give, you and your financial advisors may come up with another method of giving that could better suit your overall aims.

Board Members

Most nonprofits have volunteer boards that oversee the organization. The board members are generally active in the community that is being served by the nonprofit. To a large degree, board members provide avenues for outreach into the community in addition to advising the nonprofit's management team. Most board members donate to the organizations they serve and are quite deeply involved in fund-raising activities. They seem to be, by their nature, very approachable and are often excellent contacts for learning more about the organization they represent.

Volunteers

Most nonprofits have a cadre of volunteers who also know quite a bit about the organization. They, too, can be extremely helpful in explaining what the nonprofit's goals are and how it accomplishes those objectives.

Paid Solicitors

We do not see paid solicitors as being a good source of objective information.

Publications

Most of the material that we have come across relating to financial matters has to do with *acquiring* assets. We have found very little that has to do with *distributing* assets (except for spending, of course). This is oddly interesting, since every dollar that is acquired eventually has to be distributed—right?

Books

There are many, many books out there on gifting techniques, but very little is available on gifting strategies. The books we found helpful were not those that dealt directly with the issues of major gifting, but rather those that addressed the underlying issues of having wealth and making investment decisions. Most of the books published by the fund-raising industry have, not surprisingly, been written from the fund-raiser's point of view. They focus on the techniques of fund-raising, the mechanics of running a nonprofit, the management of nonprofit boards, and guidelines for grantmaking. It is largely insider material that is interesting in a general way, but we didn't find it to be very helpful from a donor's point of view.

Magazines and Newspapers

We have found that articles in magazines and newspapers vary greatly in their value. True, we did discover some helpful material on occasion, but in general, there wasn't all that much that was helpful to us. In fact, articles can sometimes be quite misleading. Our major concern here is that financial articles tend to assume that the reader fits some "average" profile. Seldom do the writers emphasize the critical need to tailor your choices to your basic situation and your personal goals, which may vary considerably from the "average."

We have noted a great sameness in the articles we've read. Many simply reiterate the "conventional wisdom" and the basic "rules of thumb" of personal financial management. That may be a good place to start, but typically this kind of material emphasizes the acquisition of assets. Rarely do you find articles that explore the options for distributing assets.

Popular financial magazines are certainly good for entertainment on long airplane flights. But they are largely preoccupied with short-term (and debatable) advice on buying stocks and mutual fund shares. ("These are the stocks to buy now!" "The year's most profitable mutual funds!") There are occasionally some thoughtful background articles in those magazines, but you really have to search for them.

The more serious business magazines may offer articles that can be helpful for estate planning and related major gifting. We have found it useful to subscribe to two or three of these magazines and scan them for pertinent articles. Every now and then we stumble over a helpful one, and the nuggets of wisdom we uncover more than compensate for the cost of the subscriptions.

Groups, Seminars, and Consultants

As we worked our way through the gifting process, we learned that there are special-interest groups cropping up around the country that bring current and would-be donors together to discuss the issues of major gifting. It is great to sort out the pros and cons of various approaches with like-minded people; we hope this trend will continue and grow. At present, these groups can be hard to find because many current and potential major donors are not enthusiastic about making themselves known. There are also consultants and paid seminars available to help donors with their plans for major gifting.

We don't know enough about these sources to be able to give a specific referral or recommendation one way or the other.

The Internet

Every indication is that the Internet is becoming the media of choice for sharing knowledge about many niche interests, including philanthropy. There is already a fair amount of information available regarding philanthropy, and it is likely that the exchange of facts and opinion will continue to grow. Any specific Internet addresses that we might share with you would certainly be obsolete by the time you read this book. So, boot up your computer, go to your favorite search engine, and see where "philanthropy" leads you. Your local librarian can probably be quite helpful if you need to brush up on how to do productive online research.

Summary Thoughts

So, where should you turn for comprehensive advice? Good question. We can only encourage you to remain open to all the sources you come across and sift through the information to find what is relevant to *your* situation. As far as we know, there just isn't any condensed, comprehensive, and straightforward body of information on major gifting issues from the donor's point of view.

If you work at it—and are as lucky as we have been—you will find legal, accounting, and money-management professionals who relate to the "soft" side (family matters, ease of administration, and so on) of gifting. They can work with you to create an overall plan that meets your objectives as a major donor. We have found our fee-paid professional advisors to be our key sources of objective information on major-gifting issues.

5
Finding the Right Professionals

PROFESSIONAL ADVISORS deal with technical issues, so why didn't we put this material in the technical section? Although these professionals handle the technical side of things, the *relationship* you have with them is often very personal. This is particularly true if you want your professional advisor to be helpful in working out issues pertaining to major gifting—an inherently personal subject. As we observe throughout this book, many professionals focus entirely on saving taxes, preserving wealth, and the like, and they may find the client who really wants to give money away to be a bit hard to relate to.

In any case, your lawyer will likely know about your private life (both financial and personal) like no one else. Your accountant will know your financial life like no one else but the IRS. Likewise, a financial planner can only be truly helpful if he or she knows all about your assets and your financial objectives. Thus, selecting and working with professional advisors is a very personal matter indeed.

Why the Preoccupation with Professionals?

We focus on finding the right professional advisors—particularly the right lawyers and accountants—because any major gifting that is undertaken to gain a tax benefit or that entails

long-term trust or estate work takes you into lawyer and accountant country. You might say, "I just want to give some
money away—I don't want to get involved with lawyers and
accountants." You can certainly do that. Just write a check
to your favorite charity and be done with it. Or donate some
appreciated stock, working directly with your broker and the
broker representing the charity. Both types of donations are
easy to do, and neither generally requires the involvement of
other professionals. Any tax benefit can be determined and
realized as you fill out your annual federal and state income-
tax forms.

If, however, you want to maximize your tax savings, take
advantage of some of the more complex gifting tools that are
available, or integrate your charitable gifting into your overall estate plan, the results are very likely to be unsatisfactory
without the knowledge and assistance of a qualified attorney
and a good financial advisor. Major gifting *is* lawyer and
accountant country.

The Lawyer and Doctor Analogy

There are a lot of parallels between choosing a doctor and
selecting a lawyer (or an accountant, broker, or financial
planner), but the differences in our attitudes can be striking.
The most fundamental difference is that most of us have had
a fair amount of experience choosing doctors, but few have
had much experience choosing lawyers. Also, we generally
choose doctors in response to a physical pain that we do not
want to live with. Any estate-related pain that might motivate us to choose a lawyer is likely to occur some time in the
future, when it's too late to create a plan that could have
avoided the problems or optimized the benefits.

The eventual pain that comes from untreated (or poorly

treated) legal matters is likely to be financial as well as emotional. In many cases this pain will not be yours to bear; instead it will be borne by our surviving families. This lack of immediate, personal motivation can make it very easy to procrastinate, putting off the process of choosing a lawyer and taking action to put your estate in order.

Another big difference between choosing doctors and lawyers is that most of us have some type of medical insurance, but as far as we know, none of us have legal insurance. We may grumble about the cost, but most of us agree to follow through with recommended medical treatment without much hesitation. And we tend not seek out the low bid or continually question the cost of each stage of that treatment. Yet with lawyers and financial professionals, because we pay the bills directly, we are much more likely to be cost-driven in our choices, and we may not follow through with the recommended course of action to completely resolve the issues in question—often to our detriment.

Let's say that you went to a new doctor who was unfamiliar with your history. If, after a short conversation, the doctor reached a diagnosis, prescribed a drug, and scheduled you for surgery, you would speak up and tell the doctor, "Wait! There's more to it than that." You would know that the doctor was treating you as a standard case and prescribing a standard treatment, clearly in a hurry to start the billing process and get you out the door. When it comes to our physical well being, we know that we are individuals and that an "average" diagnosis reached without appropriate tests and careful interviews might not only be inaccurate, but also downright dangerous.

Suppose, instead, you went to a new lawyer, unfamiliar with your overall financial picture, your desired lifestyle, and your tolerance for administrative pain. This new lawyer would not know your family relationships (not just how many kids you have, but your *relationship* with them), your goals, or your value system. If this lawyer arrived at a standard diagnosis for you, recommended a standard trust arrangement, a standard will, and a tax-saving family partnership, would you think, "Wow, what a productive meeting!" Or would you have a panic attack similar to the one you had with the doctor who reached such dramatic conclusions without appropriate testing to ensure that the recommended treatment would truly fit your situation?

Chances are you might not be too concerned, since most of us haven't been conditioned to expect a "thorough diagnosis" when we sit down with a lawyer. Although they might think nothing of getting a second opinion for a medical diagnosis, few people are likely to seek a second opinion on legal or financial advice. Sad to say, most of us would probably be relieved to find that the process was going faster (and would therefore cost less) than we had anticipated.

Administrative Issues

The administrative load that you will ultimately carry depends in large part on the nature of your relationship with your professional advisors and how *they* view administrative issues. That is, the planning sessions with your advisors will determine the long-term administrative load that you will be committed to live with.

It is normal and reasonable for a professional advisor to lean toward some of the more involved and ongoing solutions to a client's needs. It would be naive to expect otherwise. We think there are four reasons for this. First, given that tax savings are generally *the* goal of estate and gifting legal efforts and that the more complex approaches may have the potential to wring out every last dollar of potential tax saving, it is not too surprising that professionals in these fields tend to lean this way. Most lawyers are likely to assume that you, the new client just walking in the door, share this typical point of view and would agree that that saving every last tax dollar is probably what you want.

Second, the professional may not be giving as high a priority to the soft issues (simplicity of administration, sensitivity to family relationships, charitable gifting, and so on) that you may find quite important.

Third, professionals are very comfortable with the more complex aspects of their fields and (we think) tend to forget just how difficult it is for us civilians to comprehend the legal concepts that they are sharing with us.

Fourth, some advisors may instinctively choose options that will enhance their continued income. We think that most professional advisors (in every field) truly have their client's best interests in mind and that their recommendations are based on their professional judgement of what is best for their clients. But as always, some caution is in order. If, after some discussion, you get the impression that the chemistry isn't right, you should feel quite free to say, "Thank you," and move on. We think a key test for this may be to note who is doing the talking. If the professional is doing all the talking and you are doing all the listening, instead of there being a good give-and-take balance, this strikes us as a signal to be concerned.

Another issue to keep in mind when selecting your professional advisor is to remember that the best way to ensure that you will be comfortable with the approaches chosen—and the administrative arrangements that are part of these choices—is to sign up with a lawyer or other advisor whose basic style is in tune with yours. If you want "aggressive" tax advice, and you are willing to accept the ongoing administrative involvement (yours and your lawyer's) that this implies, find a lawyer and an accountant who practice in this vein. If your basic outlook is more conservative, and you would prefer a simpler administrative life for yourself and your family, then find a lawyer and an accountant who are comfortable with that approach. Otherwise, continual frustration is likely to be yours.

Even after you find a lawyer, accountant, financial planner, or fund-raiser whose style is within your comfort zone, it is wise to invest the time necessary to fully understand and evaluate the options that are open to you. After all, you and your family are the ones who will live with the administration dictated by these arrangements, and it will be you and your family who run the risk of IRS challenges.

Paying for Advice

We think that the cost of estate planning is clearly a case of "pay me now, or pay me later." There is no question that engaging professional advisors in discussions of "soft" issues such as your personal values, lifetime goals, lifestyle choices, and so on will keep the meter running for a while. There is no question that plans and documents tailored to fit a unique situation (and we are all unique) will be more costly than arrangements created by punching "enter" on a keyboard, printing out slightly modified boilerplate, and signing on the dotted line.

We are convinced that taking the time (and spending the money) up front to establish a plan that fully fits your needs and wishes will, in the long run, produce rewards for you and your family that will far outweigh the investment it took to get things right. We believe this to be true not only from a financial standpoint, but also in terms of emotional and relationship issues over the long haul.

Major Gifting Requires Expert Advice

So what's the tie-in to major gifting? Our view is that without professionals who are committed to listening to your situation and encouraging you to explore your objectives, your "diagnosis and treatment" will probably turn out to be unsatisfactory. If you truly hope to have a rewarding major-gifting experience, we urge you to find advisors who understand how charitable gifting and specific tools for that gifting fit in with your objectives and your overall planning.

We have been able to establish fine professional and personal relationships with our "business" partners, including individuals in the charitable organizations that we support. This has been possible because we have been willing to be candid about our expectations and because we have been willing to change professional partners when we have realized that our agendas did not mesh comfortably. We are not suggesting that you should try to change the way any of these advisors does business. That never works. Rather, we encourage you to be selective, working with new professional partners until you find the right fit. Once you've found it, life is good.

6
Selecting Charities to Support

OUR SEARCH FOR CHARITIES was a fairly structured process, with strong personal and emotional overtones. Your choices are likely to be different than ours, but we hope that our experience with the process will give you some ideas for your own search.

We put a lot of effort into choosing our charities. At first, it seemed that selecting them was going to be a huge chore. But as we went through the process, we found it to be quite interesting. In fact, it became somewhat of a calling.

It may seem that we were rather cold and calculating in making our choices. Cold, certainly not. Calculating, perhaps. Methodical, most definitely. In fact, we believe that a major donor has an absolute obligation to be methodical in deciding which charities to support. How else will the best interests of those in need be served?

Where to Start the Search?

We started our process by reviewing, rather informally, the mass mailings and cold calls that we regularly received. And, like just about everyone else, we found those mailings and calls to be fundamentally irritating. We were especially annoyed by mailings from organizations that we had never supported and by calls that interrupted our dinnertime. Yet, how else do "good charities" get the word out? That's certainly a quandary for many organizations, we are sure.

It is interesting to note, in retrospect, that none of the

charities that we now support came to our attention through such mailings or cold calls. We did not rule those organizations out because we didn't like their approach; it was more that their methods didn't seem to reflect a well-managed, efficient operation.

When we realized that the charities we had information on did not give us any great sense of mission, we could see that we needed to get serious about this, to get off the couch, get out into the world, and see what was really going on. We started at ground zero. We knew nobody in the nonprofit world, we had no community network to speak of, and we had no basis for judging the merits of one nonprofit over another.

Mainly we had our "baggage." That is, we had our own prejudices for and against certain charities. We knew that some of them did very well and that others had serious problems. We felt a powerful resistance to national charities that spent huge sums on the shotgun, mass-mailing approach to fund-raising, but we knew little about local organizations, beyond a few names and some vague idea of their objectives and their effectiveness.

So, we decided to venture forth and see what we could learn. That search proved to be a fascinating process.

Developing Our Criteria

As we began to explore the possibilities, we soon realized that we actually did have a fairly well-formulated set of criteria for what we were looking for. Naturally, we were guided by our personal experiences—some recent, and some that had been part of our thinking throughout our lives—and by the examples set for us by people we had come to admire.

For instance, our experiences during our daughter's illness brought us into contact with a wide range of people in the care-giving community. We have been truly touched by the extraordinary giving of time and heart from these generous people. Often salaries are not high in these professions, and many who become involved in such work are volunteers who receive no compensation at all.

These experiences led us to be very oriented toward social services organizations that are dedicated to helping those who have nowhere else to turn. In particular, we came to favor organizations that deal with people who need help now—people who are hurting, either physically or mentally. Our awareness of the extraordinary personal sacrifices made by many individuals in the caring community has led us to think in terms of "helping the helpers" in our gifting choices. We like to support those who do hands-on helping. We derive great satisfaction from directing the resource we control (money) to the individuals who work directly with people who are truly in need.

As we did our research, we came to be more comfortable with the some of the larger umbrella-type national organizations, particularly those with strong and effective local affiliates. However, in general, we have found that we are leaning more toward support of our local organizations. It is easier to know more about them, and we sense that local control leads to more efficient use of resources. (Though not always, to be sure.)

We have found that the organizations we support generally do a very good job of communicating what they are doing and how well they are doing it. It is difficult to give ongoing support to organizations that do not communicate this information well.

When we started our research, these preferences were quite subliminal. It was only later that we were able to recognize them more clearly and formalize a list of our criteria. To summarize, our criteria include:

- **Social-service orientation.** We like the environment, the arts, and so on, but our first sense of mission rests with social services.

- **Efficiently run organizations.** We feel an obligation on behalf of those in need to channel funds to the organizations that most effectively manage their operations. Simply stated, a charity that is not efficiently run is short-changing the clients it is supposed to be serving.

- **Helping the Helpers.** We want to support organizations that attract staff and volunteers who are truly dedicated to the cause, to serving the clients of the charity in whatever way they can.

- **Good Communicators.** We are comfortable supporting organizations that tell us what they do and how well they do it. We are not comfortable giving to those few that don't.

A Rewarding Adventure

So, as these criteria began to clarify in our minds, we set out to learn what the nonprofit world had to offer. Here are just a few of the interesting and productive experiences that we had.

The American Red Cross

We had been casual donors to the American Red Cross for some time, giving perhaps a hundred bucks a year or so. We had positive, World War II images of the Red Cross, and the group had been very effective in getting our son home on military emergency leave on two occasions. We liked the Red Cross. But wasn't the Red Cross one of those big, national bureaucratic outfits that we don't favor?

Our deeper involvement began when we got an invitation

to come to a dinner featuring Elizabeth Dole, a national political figure and, at that time, the President of the American Red Cross. (Hey, we're as star-struck as the next couple.) The cost was about $50 per ticket. We went, met Mrs. Dole at the pre-dinner reception, heard her speak, and were recruited. We also met some Red Cross staffers and generally had a great time. The process of researching nonprofits looked like it was going to be fairly painless.

To shorten the story a bit, we became friends of and major donors to the Red Cross. Why did we choose it? Because we related to what the Red Cross organization does, and we learned that it is highly rated for fiscal responsibility.

The Caring Pregnancy Center

Near the beginning of our search, Linda came across a guest column in the local newspaper written by Yvonne Williams, executive director of the Caring Pregnancy Center. We were both drawn to the description of their work, so Linda called and made an appointment for us to go and learn more. We met with Yvonne, learned a lot more, and have been supporters ever since.

The Caring Pregnancy Center is a local organization that works with young women who are facing crisis pregnancies. The center encourages the mothers to consider adoption or keeping the babies, as appropriate. It provides emotional, financial, and physical assistance, during and after the pregnancies. The staff are non-judgmental and non-political. The center charges no fees. It brings reasoned, quiet, in-depth, and loving "one life at a time" support to young women in the midst of what may well be the most serious crisis of their lives.

We support the center financially and do some networking on its behalf because it does work we admire and relate to. The center is largely a volunteer organization, and it accomplishes a lot with the money it receives. We enjoy the friendship of the center's caring staff and dedicated volunteers.

Cancer and Grief Support Groups

When our daughter, Sue, was sick with cancer, she joined a cancer support group in Boulder. With support she got from this group, she was able to spend her last six months living rather than dying. By this we mean that she was able to bring her naturally positive and open nature to the forefront and live positively during the time that remained to her.

Jennifer McKeown was (and is) the facilitator of this group. She makes it work, helping to bring strength, hope, and comfort to those in the grip of life's ultimate crisis. We now financially support Jennifer's work with a related grief group and with a breast cancer support group that she also facilitates.

Community Food Share

Community Food Share (CFS) is a local food bank that collects donated food and redistributes it to agencies that help feed those in need. It also has a vigorous gardening program, both producing food for those in need and helping individuals to create their own gardens and grow food for themselves. It is a largely volunteer organization and is very well run by Kathy Coyne and her staff.

We had heard good things about this group and were quite impressed with the fundamental common sense of their approach. We were modest financial supporters for a couple of years. Dick then got involved as a volunteer in warehouse planning and some administrative areas. That contact led us to know the people of the organization quite well, and we then became major financial supporters.

Other Organizations

We also support a number of other local social-service organizations that we respect and admire. Given what we have said about our criteria and our interests, the list is pretty predictable. It has gotten longer than we had originally anticipated and now includes nearly fifteen different groups plus the ones already noted. Sometimes we think the list is just too long, but it sure is hard to prune. We keep thinking that we are going to make it shorter, but somehow it just seems to keep growing.

We still don't respond to cold calls from what we think of as "telephone boiler rooms." When we get such calls from charities of one kind or another, we ask that the group send us information that we can review. They rarely do.

7
Volunteering: An Integral Part of the Process

VOLUNTEERING IS AN INTEGRAL part of our major gifting effort. As we searched for nonprofits that we wished to support financially, we also found organizations that we wished to support with our time. And as we came to know organizations more intimately as volunteers, we became more interested in supporting them financially. We have found that gifting of our time and money has, over time, become a very integrated effort, with each type of involvement enhancing the other.

We're not sure if people are joyous because they volunteer or if they volunteer because they are joyous, but there does seem to be a correlation. We have met some very interesting, outgoing, and involved people in the volunteer world. Being one of them is a privilege. We highly recommend volunteering.

Volunteering is relatively new to us. We do not have a family tradition of volunteering. Like many people, we were consumed with raising kids, tending to home matters, making a living, and so on. Linda did volunteer one day a week, for a number of years, at the hospital gift shop where we used to live, but that was about it. Dick was always busy with after-hours activities with family or pursuing hobbies. He was not drawn to volunteering.

When we retired, we talked about it in a kind of "well, we gotta do it" vein. We did not really want to, but we felt that we should. However, family events overtook our lives for the next couple of years or so. Eventually things settled down, and about the time we got into the money-distribution business, we found ourselves ready to reconsider the volunteering issue.

Thus, our plans and actions for giving time as well as money developed in parallel. It is important to point out that we began planning our financial gifting with a fairly clear sense of mission. We had no clear-cut plan in the area of personal volunteering. It evolved as time went along.

Much to our surprise, volunteering has become an important focus of our lives. We weren't motivated by pent-up energy to go out there and become volunteers; it just grew on us. Our interest was an outgrowth of our contact with organizations from the donor side.

When we started learning about volunteer opportunities, we had no real sense of the range of opportunities that were available. We just fell into things. We will share with you what we got involved with.

Unskilled Activities. By this, we mean the kind of thing where you just show up and pitch in. Dick started out not wanting much to do with these activities, but after he gave it a try a time or two, he found that he enjoyed the experience. There is a certain sense of reward that comes from just joining in and being part of the team.

Semi-Skilled Activities. Linda works four hours each week at the local library, preparing books for the shelves. She loves books and greatly enjoys the camaraderie of the library staff. She is dedicated to this commitment and makes a great effort to be there every Tuesday, as scheduled. However, given the nature of the task, she does have leeway to shift to a different day or to be absent for a week or two for a trip, without feeling guilty. In short, this volunteer job is a good fit.

Projects. This is Dick's comfort zone. He likes to take a task assignment, go home and do his work, and then come in and meet with people to review the results. Working on internal layout of the new Community Food Share facility is a good example. Dick was in his element and enjoyed the process.

Governance. By this we mean being part of a nonprofit's governing process. This can be as a member of a board, member of a planning committee, or part of a group that determines funds distribution. There are lots and lots of opportunities out there to become involved at this level. We do some of this. Probably the greatest reward to us from this type of involvement is the contact with some really interesting people.

Fund-raising. If there is one universal opportunity where volunteering is in demand by the nonprofits, it is no doubt in every aspect of fund-raising. We don't get involved much in direct fund-raising, but early on we realized that probably our special place in the charitable world was to work as behind-the-scenes missionaries for the concept of major gifting. Consequently, we have put a lot of our volunteer energy into this book. This, we suppose, is an other example of how, with some active searching among the vast number of volunteer opportunities out there, you will likely find the place that you "belong."

Personal Relationships in Volunteering. In our experience, when you donate money, the personal relationships are important, but not critical. We can comfortably give money to an organization without knowing the people well, or in many cases, without knowing them at all. In volunteering, personal relationships are more fundamental—in fact, they are crucial. This is because, when volunteering, you repeatedly go back, generally working with the same set of people. Obviously, if you don't feel comfortable with the people you work with and don't believe that the work you are doing is really worthwhile, it is unlikely that you will continue that activity over the long term. Conversely, when you like the folks you meet as a volunteer, you can develop friendships that become an important part of your life.

8
Clarifying the Process

As WE MOVED ALONG, learning what we needed to learn, we found that we were traveling through a fairly structured process. There was reason to it all. What follows is an overview of what we found to be the important elements of that process.

The Structure

Our journey toward becoming major donors has been a comprehensive process, successful in large part because we addressed the many elements as a whole. FIGURES 8-1 and 8-2 provide an overview of the process.

We think that all these issues are important in creating a rewarding plan for major gifting. We strongly suspect that you will too. As a test, look at FIGURE 8-2 and pick out any single issue that you think wouldn't be worth considering as you design a plan for giving away significant portions of your net worth. Difficult to find one, isn't it?

The process that these two charts suggest came after the fact, not before. They may present an organized, even linear process, but it didn't start out that way. In reality, a lot of things were going on at the same time. Various people and issues came into our lives for a bit, faded out for a while, and then returned. Only in retrospect were we able to view the experience in an integrated, fairly structured fashion.

Categorizing the major issues as "hard" or "soft" has been helpful to us. Hard issues are those that can be measured and compared, described in numerical terms, and clearly defined in legal or numerical language. Soft issues are those that are

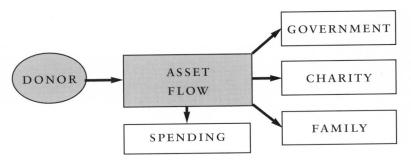

Figure 8-1: Lifetime Asset Flow
This figure shows what we see as the basic financial facts of life: What you don't spend will go to the government, to charities, and to family.

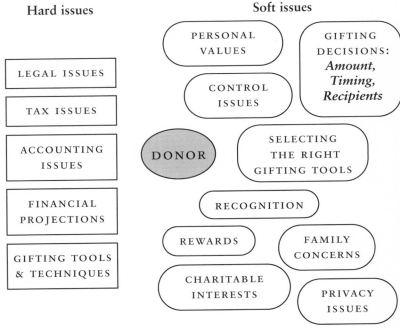

Figure 8-2: Hard and Soft Issues
This list reflects the issues and activities that swirl around the donor, making the major-gifting enterprise so very interesting. On the left are the "hard" issues—those of a generally more quantifiable nature. On the right are the "soft" issues—the more subjective issues that are often factors of the heart.

emotional, subjective, or relationship-oriented—things that do not lend themselves to measurement or clear comparison. You'll notice that we have not emphasized any one issue over another. This was intentional, because we feel that although all of the issues are important, the degree of importance rests in the mind of the individual donor.

The hard/soft distinction has helped us work out what we want to do. Understanding this distinction is especially helpful when you are dealing with professional advisors, who generally focus attention on the hard issues and devote much less time to the soft issues. (In fact, some lawyers barely acknowledge that the soft category exists.)

The Steps

As we look back, we can see that the steps we were taking could be clearly defined. We often found ourselves working on all of them at the same time. We expect that the order of anyone else's process may be somewhat different than ours, yet we believe that anyone who becomes a major donor will need to deal with roughly the same steps.

1. **Decide to take the initiative.** Taking the initiative is in many ways the hardest step. There are so many reasons not to begin. All too easily, life can go by without your ever making the effort or taking that first step.

2. **Get advice from objective advisors and sources.** There does not seem to be one nice, clear path toward basic answers, but there is certainly a great deal to be gained by seeing what knowledgeable individuals have to say about these matters.

3. **Determine your family financial projection.** As we say so many times in this book, we think that

working out a family financial projection is the key
to becoming financially confident enough to embark
on a major-gifting program.

4. **Work out the soft issues.** No doubt about it—getting
the soft issues resolved was a critical step in moving
forward.

5. **Determine the best tools to use.** There are a lot of
choices out there. The key challenge, it seems to us,
is to pick out the methods of giving (the tools and
techniques) that best fit your situation, which are not
necessarily the ones that others may think are right
for you.

6. **Select charities and give.** We've already talked about
the process of choosing the charities you want to
support. We have found that once we worked
through most of the background issues, actual giving
has been the fun part. It has not been painful at all.

You may be asking yourself, "Why not jump from Step 1
to Step 5?" If so, you're not alone. Many people think a potential major donor can effectively do that. That particular
short cut certainly would not work for us. We found a number of good reasons for going through each one of these
stages in order to get comfortable in the role of major donor.
First, it is difficult to give big dollars unless you fully understand how it will affect your long-term financial planning
and net worth. Second, getting deeply involved in the technical side (the tools and techniques for charitable gifting) too
early in the process can actually work against your desire to
give. (Digging through tools and techniques is not the fun
part.) We strongly suggest that you sort out the basic objectives and issues behind your wish to give before exploring

gifting techniques. Once we had resolved these background issues, it was much easier to choose the best tools to accomplish those goals.

Donors and Recipients

As we have said before, the money we don't spend will go to government, charity, and family—in some combination. We think of giving money to charities as "donating," giving money to family as "sharing," and giving money to the government as "giving up" the money. In the discussion that follows, we will call all three groups "recipients," for want of a catchier term. And, although "donor" may not capture some of the subtle differences in giving to these three recipient groups, we will use it here to refer to the individuals giving the money away.

As part of our effort to bring some structure to a rather rambling process, we sharpened up our understanding of just how each of these players look at money. As always, we must deliver our broad assessments with a healthy dose of over-generalization.

The Donor's View on Money

The easiest option is for donors to simply hang on to their money until they die and leave it to family, charity, and the government at that time. Naturally, recipients would prefer that donors turn the money over to them sooner rather than later, allowing them to manage and use it.

Tax implications greatly complicate this dilemma. Much of the intelligent gifting process consists of resolving these conflicting issues. Let's take a look at all the recipients and their agendas in more detail.

The Recipients' Views on Money

Government. Governmental bodies seem to have two tax-related priorities. First, they want the tax money now for payment of government expenses, but sometimes they will accept it later. The second priority is a social agenda, whereby tax policy is used to encourage some behaviors and discourage others. Determinations of which behaviors are good or bad are, or course, quite subjective, and these decisions are buffeted by the political winds of the times.

For example, current government tax policy rewards charitable gifting (to a point) by allowing tax deductions for it, while levying taxes on gifting (beyond a point) to family or friends. There certainly are some "redistribution of wealth" concepts built into the tax code. Note that we view these realities as political neutrals. They are the reality, and that is what we deal with.

Charities. Most charities need the money, and they would prefer to have it now. However, they are also happy to accept it later—at your death, perhaps. They have two reasons to want the money now: First, they need to cover current operating expenses. Second, they might use it to make long-term investments that will help cover future needs (endowments). If your donation is earmarked for their endowment fund, they will definitely want to get the money now, so that they can begin to invest it for future growth and income and also (we expect) to ensure that the money actually comes to them.

Friends and Family. In most instances, family and friends would also like the money now. Current needs always loom large. And, given the choice, they would prefer to have the assets in their possession rather than in that vague, "well, maybe someday" category.

What does this all mean for your planning for charitable gifting? Quite a lot, really. It is helpful to keep in mind how your potential recipients are thinking about the money that you are thinking of giving them. This sensitivity (well, sensitivity for family, friends, and the charities anyway) might have an impact on the how and the when of your gifting plans.

9
Business Issues

WE THINK THERE ARE TWO core business issues that have a lot to do with whether a gifting program will be a rewarding experience or a chore. The most fundamental one is, of course, basic financial analysis—understanding how gifting or not gifting will effect your financial situation over the long term. We feel this is so important, in fact, that all of Section 3 is about the role of financial analysis in the gifting process.

The second core business issue is the more subtle matter of the administrative load that may come with tax-efficient charitable and family gifting. This chapter speaks first to the administrative issues and then highlights some of the key financial analysis issues.

Complexity and Administration

You might think that this discussion belongs in Section 2: The Technical Side. Not really. Complexity and administration are very personal issues. The complexity and administration responsibilities that you build into your estate and gifting plans will have a direct and major impact on how you'll be spending your time for the rest of your life. What could be more personal than that?

Winding up a complex estate has given us a priceless education in the need to keep an estate as simple as possible. As one lawyer said to us, "A simple estate is very expensive"—meaning that if you don't use some of the more-involved estate-planning tools, the tax man will take an exorbitant amount of your net worth at death. That's true, but as we have learned, there can be a happy medium.

Our experience with the "dark side" of complex estate arrangements has had a profound effect on how we view everything related to estate and financial planning. And that includes how we address major gifting.

We have found that the key to keeping a comprehensive, quantified view of the many issues involved in managing an estate is to make each of the individual issues as simple as possible. Like so many of the points made in this book, this is such basic common sense that it may seem too trivial to mention. Yet the forces working to make our lives more complicated are both pervasive and intrusive.

We learned that we couldn't do major gifting unless we were able to see how it would balance with the rest of our financial, legal, and personal factors, and it is difficult to see the balance of things when the different elements get too complicated. Major gifting can add some complications of its own. If you aren't careful, at some point it may begin to seem like too much trouble. That has a lot to do with overall estate planning; it is also relevant to tax-efficient gifting.

Our experience has been that the well-intended donor can accomplish major gifting in a tax-efficient way without having to use the more "aggressive" or more complicated tax techniques. By the way, when a lawyer says a technique is "aggressive," it means that the odds of some conflict with the IRS are reasonably high. Some lawyers seem to relish such challenges. We don't.

The problem is that many of the approaches to estate planning, money management, and gifting can look so appealing as individual projects, taken out of context, but they can quickly become overpowering when taken as a whole. There is a real potential here for the administration of your affairs to turn into an onerous burden. If you aren't careful, you may find it so hard to understand your own affairs that you won't feel comfortable doing major gifting.

What's the solution to creeping complexity and all its attendant evils? We suggest that you remember the old adage "Just because you can, it does not mean you should." Feel free to walk away from any proposed technique that you think you might be uncomfortable administering over the years. You may need to occasionally remind your professional advisors of your views on this issue.

As a footnote, we have had experiences with lawyers who believed that any technique that could produce tax savings should *automatically* be implemented. Never mind the cost of using that technique, the amount of money and time it would take to administer, the risks it might pose of being audited, the ongoing flood of paperwork it would generate, or (most important) the potential it might hold for creating family conflicts. We no longer work with those folks.

Legal arrangements take maintenance because tax laws change, court cases change the interpretation of existing laws, and family situations change. Any legal agreement that you make must be periodically reviewed to ensure that the original intent is still being served by existing arrangements. Likewise, most funded trust arrangements require annual tax returns, and many require you to make ongoing investment decisions. As basic arrangements become more complex, keeping up with your administrative responsibilities can become quite a burden. Keeping the basic legal arrangements as simple as possible will help minimize the amount of maintenance required.

Financial Analysis

We can just hear you saying, "Oh my, they're going to start talking about tax rates, deductions, and spreadsheets." No, not yet. (You will find that in Section 3.) What we are talking about here is the necessity, for us, of having the underlying financial analysis in order to feel comfortable with major gifting.

How Much Is Enough?

It seems clear that folks who are not confident that they are fiscally secure are very unlikely to become major donors. Having a good understanding of your projected net worth can provide reassurance that you will have enough to meet your needs and open the door for considering major gifting during your lifetime. We all need to be sure that we will have enough money as we live out our lives.

So how much is "enough?" A tough question. (Don't hold your breath, we have no magic answers here.) And is this ever a question where a generalized "rule of thumb" answer is inadequate! We're convinced that the answers to "How much is enough?" and the related question "How much can we give?" are deeply personal and very dependent on each individual's financial situation and lifestyle. On a more basic level, the answers will also reflect each person's inner makeup and need for financial reserves.

We have been able to reach a conclusion on how much is "enough" for us. Having this baseline in mind helps our gift planning process immeasurably. In short, financial analysis has been a fundamental step in becoming major donors.

The Volatility Problem

We now have a good handle on our financial situation. We have money management support that we have confidence in, and we understand the nature of the stock market quite well. We know that it goes up and down—a lot. We understand volatility.

So, given stock market losses or gains (depending on the

day you read this), international economic problems, and political instabilities, we should be able to slide through the ups and downs without a care, right? Well, no, not really. It may be fun to watch the markets go up, but it is not at all entertaining to watch them go down. The downs make us very nervous.

Without our ability to go back and look at our long-term plan and see that we are still financially on track, we would be tempted to back away from our major-gifting initiatives. But we can review our spreadsheets and know that we can continue to give at the level we had planned. We find that our long-term financial analysis gives us the confidence to sustain our gifting plan even as we observe significant volatility in our investment values.

Can We Afford It?

We often find that when it comes time to make a major gift, we regress back to our "Can we really afford it?" frame of mind. It is so easy to lose sight of the "big picture." Even though we have now been through this cycle many times, we often need some reassurance that, yes, we can afford to give away this amount of money.

Is this because we can't really accept how much we are worth? Perhaps. In fact, we think a lot of people have that problem. We all know someone who has a sense that there may never be enough, that it might all go away. We see it frequently in the generation that grew up during the Great Depression, where most families struggled and real suffering was a fact of life.

But this type of unease is also a large factor for many of us who are somewhat younger that that. Many of us can remember years when money was tight—when we lived in apartments over garages, kept the clunker going for two more years, and looked for really cheap motels when we traveled with our family. Most of us have gone through periods of employment instability. We suspect these earlier life experiences have a real impact on our sense of financial well being (or lack of it) throughout our lives. For many of us, it can be hard to break away from the ingrained sense that $100 is a really big deal. The secret to keeping this issue in prospective is having a good strategic financial analysis in the background that helps us see our gifting amounts in relation to our overall wealth.

Family Financial Projection

Knowing our numbers has been the key to establishing the personal confidence we needed to begin and to sustain our major gifting. Financial analysis has served us well in quantifying what we can give. It has helped us to view our financial situation in a more factual way, rather than in a somewhat fear-based way. It is the basis for being comfortable with our major gifting. As part of our planning process, we have developed a computer spreadsheet that does a great job of providing the information you'll need. We'll share it with you in Section 3.

10
Recognition and Reward

WE HAVE COME TO SEE an important distinction between the terms "recognition" and "reward." Recognition is, by definition, a process of bringing attention to the donors for their good works. In effect, it says to the world, "these people did this good thing." And that may be a positive thing to do—in some cases.

The concept of reward is a much more subtle thing. We think it describes an inner feeling of satisfaction. It is the sense that donors get of having done a good thing, of helping to make a difference in areas for which they have a passion. This inner sense of reward can be totally independent of any form of public recognition.

As a note to our friends in the fund-raising business, this is powerful distinction—not a just a nuance or an arcane bit of semantics. We know that many donors and potential donors are like us, in that they truly seek that inner sense of reward that comes from seeing that their donations are making a difference, while viewing public recognition as a neutral or even a negative factor.

Recognition

Receiving recognition for the money and time you donate to a nonprofit is an interesting subject. There is a lot of diversity in the types of recognition that people might seek out. For example, businesses tend to want and need public recognition for their charitable efforts; that recognition may even be their main reason for giving. We support this enthusiastically. Giving them the recognition they need is a small price to pay for what are often major contributions. In fact, it would be great to have more commercial gifting and related publicity.

For individuals, recognition is a far more complicated issue, one that is entirely dependent on individual points of view. It must be a difficult task for nonprofits to figure out the best way to recognize their individual donors. We think that nonprofits would reap some big benefits if they took the time to understand the difference between recognition and reward, and then determined which one individual donors would respond best to.

Many people have very good reasons for not wanting the public to know that they are donors. There may be family or business reasons, issues with neighbors, or security concerns; they may not want their names on fund-raising lists; or they may simply not want to share any part of their private financial situation with the general public. Sometimes fund-raisers seem to have a difficult time realizing that fear of unwanted publicity may give some people a legitimate and decisive reason not to give.

Public and Private Recognition

In our case, we find public recognition somewhat painful. We are retiring by nature and neither seek nor enjoy the limelight. Now, that statement does seem to conflict with the fact that this book exists—talk about public recognition, and self-generated at that. Although our strong convictions have led us to create this book in hopes of encouraging others to become major donors, it in no way negates the fact that public recognition is generally uncomfortable for us.

We do appreciate private recognition. We enjoy getting a personal note from someone we know in a nonprofit that we give money to. It is very rewarding to walk into the facility of a nonprofit that we support and know the people we see there.

Is there some contradiction in all of this? Perhaps, but we think it comes down to this. In our case, we really want the organizations we support to know us as individuals, and we would prefer the general public to not know us at all. Is this a typical outlook? We don't know. It probably varies tremendously.

Gifts, plaques, recognition dinners, and the like are a mixed blessing. Generally we feel better when the charity dedicates its funds to its mission and goes easy on gifts or plaques for donors. For volunteers, plaques seem like a very good thing, since most of us may be more comfortable being recognized for our donations of time than for our donations of money. In our case, it's easy to imagine hanging a plaque on the wall that recognizes our volunteering, but it's pretty unlikely that we'd be comfortable doing the same thing with a plaque recognizing a gift of money.

Annual dinners are enjoyable to us if their basic mission is celebration of the organization's work and its mission, with individual donor recognition as a very secondary aspect. Of course, charities generally *like* to give public recognition and may be quite disappointed if a major donor does not want to join in.

Nonprofits really do appreciate the support of those who help fund their activities, and they want to do what they can to express their thanks. They also like to share the fact that they have a wide range of donors because it may help boost their ongoing fund-raising efforts.

Confidentiality

We have given a lot of thought to this issue of confidentiality. Sometimes valuable doors have been opened to us through the knowledge gained from other donors going public, allowing their stories to be told in the local newspaper. We appreciate that they allowed it to happen because our own charity-related interests have been well-served by their willingness to make themselves known.

But do we want to do this? As you can tell, we are in somewhat of a quandary about it. We tend to go along with being on the public list if we think it might really be helpful to the charity if we stand up and allow ourselves to be counted. But, in general, we remain uncomfortable with it.

Rewards

We have been doing major gifting for a number of years now. Long enough to begin to feel a real sense of reward from some of our choices, and long enough to look back and see how our thoughts and convictions on major gifting developed through our actions. Each situation is different, but we are heartened to see that the basics of our approach have been quite consistent. We have managed to strive for simplicity, give tax savings its proper priority, seek counsel from our professional advisors, and seek approaches that fit our situation. Here is a sampling of how some of the gifting decisions have worked out.

The Red Cross Story

As noted earlier, we are major donors to the American Red Cross. We support it because it is a large organization that manages its resources well, dealing effectively with disasters of all types. It is an efficient organization, focused on the prevention and mitigation of disasters. The Red Cross makes effective use a large number of well-trained, experienced, and dedicated volunteers on a local, national, and international basis.

Supporting the Red Cross gives us a great sense of giving a hand to those who find themselves, when disaster strikes, with nowhere else to turn, whether they are suffering the after-effects of a house fire just down the street or an earthquake in a far off Third World country. The Red Cross is there to alleviate the kind of human suffering that strikes so suddenly.

We know a number of the people in our local Red Cross chapter. In fact, our Red Cross friends were the first to urge us to step forward and explain how we approach major gifting. For a while, we were quite involved in the governance side of the local chapter. Being part of the Red Cross has been a first-rate learning experience, and we wouldn't have missed it for the world. Even though we are now working with other nonprofits on the governance side, we continue to be major financial supporters of the Red Cross.

The Community Foundation Story

Early in our search for the right charities, Linda noted in the paper that a local businesswoman had made a very substantial donation to the local Community Foundation. We had never heard of a Community Foundation, so we called Josie Heath, executive director of the local organization. Hers was a familiar name in our community. We met with her and a couple of the organization's board members. We learned a great deal about Community Foundations in general and were impressed.

We then basically went our own way for three years. We still needed to go through a learning process to discover what all was out there in the world of nonprofits. But then, we came back. By then, we had learned much more about nonprofits, about ourselves, and about what a Community Foundation had to offer us.

We have a developed a great deal of respect for the community-foundation concept and for this Community Foundation in particular. It may sound a little odd, but we have found it to be the most balanced nonprofit organization that we have become involved with. It truly views the community as a whole, looking for creative ways to bring donors, skilled volunteers, and nonprofit groups together to find ways to satisfy everyone's needs.

We have selected the local Community Foundation to be the beneficiary of Dick's tax-deferred retirement plan, should he die prematurely. We have funded an advised fund with them that will have the dual purpose of supporting regional charities over the long run and creating an opportunity for a younger family member to become involved with philanthropy

In the years ahead, we will probably be channeling most of our annual gifting to local charities through the Community Foundation. Working with the Community Foundation is proving to be a rewarding experience on every level.

The Community Food Share Story

We have also noted the experience of getting involved with Community Food Share, a local nonprofit food bank. Our experience with this group has also been unique and exceptionally rewarding.

Along with some volunteering, we have become steadily more involved as donors. We make a yearly donation (unrestricted, since it is good to remember that someone has to pay the phone bill). Because we are so involved with the food bank's operations, we have, on a few occasions, been able to identify some key needs, step in, and fund an essential piece of equipment. In the beginning, our funding was always done on an anonymous basis, but as we became more at home with the staff, we realized that keeping secrets wasn't worth the trouble it took. Now all the staff knows we are major donors, in addition to being volunteers, and it doesn't seem to hinder things at all.

The staff and some of the board members we work with have become good friends. As far as recognition, we have a good balance here. The staff knows what we are up to, but our name doesn't stand out in the public newsletter. That's our preference and Community Food Share respects it.

We enjoy working with the people at Community Food Share. They are a hard-working, dedicated, joyous, irreverent group that does a fine job helping those in need throughout the county (largely the working poor and some of the elderly). We enjoy being financial supporters, helping to turn donations of food and funds into an important part of the community's safety net for those in serious need of assistance.

In 1998, the food bank was able to move into a brand new building that will make it possible to more effectively serve the community at large for many years to come. The project was completed on time and within budget. The building has been well-designed, inside and out. It is tailored to today's needs, but has been built to accommodate growth and to support the expansion of some key services. Overall, it represents an outstanding collective community effort to help a fine organization go forward to serve those in need. We feel privileged and rewarded to have been part of it.

An integral part of the design is the listing, on the outside of the building, of the major donors who helped make the project possible. And there are a lot of them. When we got a letter a asking if we would like to be included, somewhat to our surprise, we said we would. We really enjoy having been part of this success and appreciate the honor of being able to "stand up" with the others who made it possible. Now, how's that for inconsistency? Maybe the phrase "part of the group" is the key factor here.

The Jill Story

We have talked about the charity and family-gifting side of being major donors. We'd like to add a bit about the rewards of giving to friends.

Jill and our daughter, Sue, were best friends from pre-kindergarten days. They met over tricycles at age four. Although Jill moved to Florida when both girls were in the sixth grade, they remained best friends, always. Jill married early, had two kids, and became a stay-at-home mom. Sue went the route of college, career, and competition in the workplace. (Sue married and had her child some 10 years later.) Jill and Sue took part in each other's weddings. They visited back and fourth. They giggled. They were so alike and so different, and they were always the best of friends.

Jill's life centers around her great husband, Steve, a marvelous family, and plenty of hard work. Money is tight. Jessica and Jason are bright, joyous, outgoing, terrific kids. College material, yes. But was college really a probability? A tough go, most likely.

As Sue's health deteriorated, she asked that we do one thing. She asked that we ensure that Jill and Steve's kids would have the opportunity to go to college. After Sue died, her husband joined with us in moving forward on her request. We spent a lot of time discussing how best to go about it with our lawyer, Kathleen, working to find the right solution.

We explored Crummey trusts (a technique for transferring money to minors in a tax-advantaged way). We weighed the pluses and minuses of the Transfer to Minors Act. We talked about other trust arrangements that would enhance control and save on taxes. We acknowledged that outright gifting of the money might undermine the potential for Jill's kids to qualify for some kinds of scholarships. But mostly, we pondered how to do this without being intrusive and undermining Jill's family relationships.

Then one day, Kathleen gave us some of the best legal advice we have ever gotten. She said, "Just give it to them." And that's just what we're doing. We have transferred assets to an account set up by Jill and Steve, in their name. At our suggestion, they established this account with the money-management firm that we work with, but the funds are theirs, not controlled by us in any way.

This is working very well. The kids know all about it and are part of it. They love it. The money is there, "in the bank;" it's not an abstraction. Jill and Steve own the money, and they retain the control that parents ought to have. It is a family thing. They keep in touch with us, letting us know how the kids are doing in school and how the college-selection visits are going. (We didn't ask for this, but we love it.)

Now, let's address some of the questions you probably have about this arrangement. Are we using our money to replace a daughter we lost? Are we intruding in another family's affairs? Are we buying love and affection? Are we undermining Jill and Steve's parental authority? We think not. Obviously, we have given a great deal of thought to such issues or we would not have brought them up. There may be some subtle impacts here, but to the best of our judgment, the advantages of making this happen far outweigh any discernible disadvantages—by a factor of about a thousand to one.

Are we worried that Jill and Steve might borrow from the college account for short-term cash-flow needs and not be able to pay it back? No. We know Jill and Steve, and we're sure that is not going to happen. Are there more tax-advantaged ways to do this? Perhaps, but in this case, a straightforward relationship is far more important than some possible tax savings. Are we recommending that others do something like this in the same way? No, not at all. This arrangement is right for this situation, these personalities, at this point in time. Other people's situations will require different solutions.

Our point, of course, is that with thought, patience, qualified advice, and an open mind, we were able to do a good thing in a way that is working very well for everyone involved. We feel good about it. We have honored Sue's request. We have lifted a burden from the shoulders of some very good friends of ours. We have helped some marvelously able and motivated young people to take a big step toward realizing their dreams. And we have done it in a simple, direct way that has no discernible drawbacks. This action gives us a tremendous sense of reward.

So What Does It Mean to Us— Or to You?

We thought about trying to summarize what these examples mean for us. Then we decided that further words were likely to be redundant. But in the end, we couldn't resist.

We think these examples show what an evolutionary process becoming major donors has been for us: getting the tax issue in its proper place in the grand scheme of things; becoming comfortable with some public knowledge of our philanthropy; and learning the profound difference between recognition and reward. We've also seen the rewards of working with our professional advisors to develop appropriate solutions to gifting issues and learning how well-conceived gifting to friends can be very rewarding to everyone concerned. We've been surprised to discover how early contacts might lie dormant for a number of years and then resurface as critical elements in the developing process.

Most of all, we feel privileged to have learned that it *is* possible to be both smart and caring, to the benefit of donor and recipient alike.

One More Story

We introduced you to Jennifer back in Chapter 6. You may remember that she was the facilitator of the cancer support group that our daughter, Sue, attended. You may also remember that we have come to know Jennifer quite well and recognize the remarkable talent she has for helping others bring their inner strengths to bear on their life crises.

Some months after Sue's death and after we knew that an inheritance was on the way, we decided that Jennifer needed to have a copy machine. Yes, a copy machine. Jennifer is a therapist with a group and a private practice—a small business, you might say. We had joked with Jennifer about the difficulty of running an operation based on communication without benefit of a copy machine. So we took $800, bought one, and took it to her home. Jennifer was quite overwhelmed. Like so many in the human services and caregiving fields, she lives mostly on the giving side of things, rarely, if ever, being on the receiving side of anything, except an inner sense of reward.

Now, you might say, a copy machine, big deal. What place does this modest experience have in the process? A big place, as it turned out. This gift was the very beginning of our odyssey. It was our first baby step. It was the first time we had ever given anything of consequence to anybody outside of our family. It felt right. We knew we were being useful to someone dedicated to helping others.

Looking back, we remember that we first hesitated to do it because the gift would not be tax deductible. It is rather embarrassing to think that we actually hesitated to "do the right thing" because of the tax code. We have since gotten past letting tax factors override our conscience.

As the months and years went by, we gained a better understanding of our net worth and became more comfortable with the concept of giving. Eventually we assumed the role of supporting Jennifer's work with the local grief group, and we have continued to do so. (This gifting is tax deductible, since it has been arranged through the auspices of a Denver nonprofit.)

Later, we learned that Jennifer was serving as volunteer facilitator for a breast cancer support group at the local hospital. The group, which had been started by a few recovering breast cancer patients, had grown to 18 participants. Jennifer had come on board as group facilitator, but there was some question about whether she could continue to do this. (Even extremely caring and giving people have to make their mortgage payments.)

We felt this was another activity that we would like to support. It was clear that a large number of people would benefit greatly from whatever we could do. Along with Jennifer, we approached the Executive Director of the Hospital Foundation to see if it would be willing to act as the funding administrator for this effort. The foundation was pleased to agree. That made the donations (ours and the donations of others) tax deductible, and it folded the business side into the existing foundation administrative structure, which gave Jennifer an efficient billing and payment process.

Working through the Hospital Foundation has made it possible for the support group to have a degree of "official" status, which we feel enhances its credibility and its chances for continuity. The foundation lets us know, on an annual basis, the status of the support account, and we make a stock gift each year to keep it funded.

For a long time, we didn't know anyone in the group personally, yet we felt a great rapport with each of them. After a couple of years of being encouraged by Jennifer to let ourselves be known to the group, we agreed. We have since received some incredibly moving notes from members of the group thanking us for our support.

Just a few weeks ago, we were at a picnic with members of the group, their spouses, kids, and significant others. We had held back because we did not want to intrude. Our concerns about this proved unnecessary. We felt comfortable and welcome. It was a fine opportunity to meet some really inspiring people. Victims? Certainly not. Strong people, bringing every resource to support their cause? Absolutely.

It is difficult to find the words to express the inner sense of reward that we get from being part of such an incredibly effective activity.

THE
TECHNICAL
SIDE

11

Taxes: Tools and Techniques

THIS SECTION DEALS WITH the technical side of major gifting. It has to do with *how effectively you give.* In particular, we will deal with how you can get *the best tax breaks, with the least amount of expense and hassle* in the process of doing your major gifting, and how you can *gift in a way that still gives you the degree of control you prefer.*

A Methodical Look at the Choices

The technical side of major gifting is often presented and perceived as a choice among complex options that will require a potential donor to become embroiled in a frustrating bramble of details as sort of an initiation. The technicalities of gifting can easily be perceived as a barrier to moving forward and enjoying the rewards of gifting.

We will strive to present the basics of major gifting in a methodical way, starting with the most straightforward methods and moving up the scale to the more financially sophisticated techniques. We hope this will give you a good overview of the world of tax-effective gifting and some idea of the control options that are available.

You will need this kind of general background in order to work effectively with your professional advisors. You may be surprised to find that you can give quite effectively, enjoy good tax benefits, and retain the degree of control you want without having to become deeply involved in the more complex side of major-giving techniques.

Even though this material is an overview written by laymen for laymen (with professional oversight), some of it can be pretty mind-numbing. If you are at the initial stage, just beginning to think about major gifting, we suggest that you scan this section and come back later and dig into it, once you have developed more of an idea of what your personal plan for giving may be.

If you are farther along in the process and have begun to select gifting tools and techniques, we hope you will find this material helpful in bringing a sense of organization to the technical issues that you are becoming embroiled in.

Why the Preoccupation with Taxes?

Tax implications can have a tremendous impact on how you gift. They certainly do in our case. The way we give has a major impact on how much of the gifting dollar gets to the intended person or activity. The federal government has provided a number of tax-advantaged gifting options for transferring money to family, as well as a number of tax- advantaged options for transferring money to nonprofits. By making use of these clearly designated options, we ensure that our gifting is much more effective than it might otherwise be. We believe there are two specific reasons for a heavy focus on taxes.

Efficiency of Distributing Funds

We feel that the well-run nonprofits are much better at serving the interests of the causes we support than the government agencies that would otherwise get our "donations" as part of their general funds. Of $1,000 that you give to a top-tier non-profit, perhaps 85 to 90% actually reaches the intended person or activity, with the remaining 10 to 15% going to administrative and fund-raising costs. If you send the same $1,000 through the general tax system, as little as 10% or less (please substitute your estimate here) may actually reach the causes that you feel are worthy of your support.

The More We Save, the More We Can Give

The second reason it makes sense for us to be preoccupied with taxes is, plain and simple, that it makes our gifting dollars go farther. That is, if we can give our $1,000 in such a way that it saves us $300 in taxes, then we have an extra $300 to give. To the recipient, that extra $300 is something very real.

It is important to remind readers that increasing our net worth is not one of our objectives and that isn't why we strive for tax savings. Quite the contrary—our goal is to hold or even decrease our net worth, during our lifetime, so that estate taxes will be minimized. Giving during our lifetimes helps others while it moves us closer to that goal.

Gifting Tools and Techniques

The selection of appropriate tools and techniques is a central part of the serious gifting process. By "tools and techniques," we mean those methods that are used to optimize tax savings and to establish a desired degree of control over the gifting process.

Of all the elements of the major gifting process, this has been the most difficult for us to learn about, to get organized in our own minds, and to document for this book. We can point to a number of reasons for this. First, there are an almost infinite number of variations to deal with, both in the tools themselves and in the individual donor situations. Second, there seems to be little out there in the literature that deals with this subject in a methodical, structured way.

Yes, there are plenty of books that discuss these tools in painful detail, but that only obscures any attempt on a layman's part to get a sense of the big picture. And, from what we have seen, newspaper and magazine articles tend to describe individual tools in a kind of "cheerleader" mode, championing the merits of one tool or another, generally out of context with the overall gifting process.

Third, the tools situation is a moving target.

The Moving Target

The IRS (which is the keeper of the toolbox) is constantly modifying the rules. This makes any summary of tools a fragile document indeed. Yet we invite you to forge ahead, since you most likely could use some type of a summary of the basic techniques, in layman's form, to help you work through the tool decision process.

So, with these cautions in mind, are the next few chapters and the calculations in them really worth your time? Absolutely. What we are after here is a sense of overall policy and strategy. We're talking about an overview that can be useful in picking a general direction. For planning purposes, we have assumed that the basic policies of governmental taxation are likely to remain in place even though there will always be ongoing modification of the details.

The details of tax law have great importance when it comes to the implementation of your plan—that moment when you actually initiate action and sign the relevant financial and legal documents. That is the point in the process where it is absolutely necessary to have skilled legal and accounting counsel, expert in current tax law and how it should be interpreted, and knowledgeable about your specific situation.

Simplicity and Linearity of the Tool Selection Process

It seems that many professionals in this industry—the fundraisers, lawyers, accountants, and financial managers—have a tendency to jump automatically to the more complex approaches to reducing taxes while doing charitable and family gifting. It would be wonderful if instead they took their clients through the choices in a methodical way, from the simple to the sophisticated, in order to arrive at a choice that best fits each client's specific situation.

We think our interests have been best-served by taking this approach—considering the simplest approaches first, moving up the complexity scale, and stopping when we reach the method that best meets our needs.

Taxes and the IRS

In this section, we'll provide an overview of IRS tax deductions and penalties—in about two pages. Need we mention that there is some simplification at work here? Legal advice it is not. It is, however, a pretty good framework from which to start viewing the options that are open to you.

Tax Rewards and Deductions

The IRS has two categories for regulating taxes in relation to gifting. In the case of *charitable gifting*, it gives you a tax reduction as a reward for making a gift—with some very specific limits. In the case of gifting to *family and friends*, it imposes a tax penalty if you give too much.

Types of Taxes

There are four types of taxes that are important to the gifting process. These are the taxes that you are seeking to minimize.

- **Income taxes.** This is (like you didn't know) the tax you pay on the amount you earn from salaries, wages, Social Security, dividends, and the like. Income from a business falls into this category.

- **Capital gains taxes.** These are taxes on the growth of

your investments. Generally these taxes come due when you sell the investment and "realize" the gain.

* **Estate taxes.** This is the tax that your estate pays to the government, based on the value of your estate at the time you die.

* **Interest and penalties.** The purist would, of course, not consider these as taxes, but there is some merit in considering them as such. You pay interest or penalties whenever your federal and state taxing agencies look at what you have done and say "Sorry, you didn't do it right. Now you get to pay us the tax you thought you weren't going to have to pay, plus accrued interest on those back taxes and a punitive penalty for being so dumb or so sly."

Dealing with the IRS

Our personal experience with the IRS has been fairly limited and uniformly unpleasant. On two occasions we have been invited to get to know the IRS more intimately. In all fairness, we probably invited ourselves into the IRS's cross-hairs by our own (or our family's) doing. These experiences have had a profound impact on how we have come to view any arrangements we might set up where the IRS or state taxing bodies might eventually be a factor.

Our first experience with the IRS took place many years ago, when we made a mistake in transferring some money from one employer's retirement program to another employer's program, during a job change. We had someone who "did our taxes," but we did not have a good ongoing relationship with a qualified CPA. Big mistake.

Anyway, we made the transfer, everything went just fine, and we forgot about it. Three years later we received a notice from the IRS stating that we owed back taxes, interest, and penalties. It was quite a sum. We had made a mistake, no question about it, and now we were about to get a chance to learn how expensive that could be.

Neither the employer transferring the money, the employer that received the money, nor the person who prepared our taxes picked up on the error. We now know that it is naive to expect any of them to have caught it, since none had access to the full information that would have been necessary to spot the problem. It never occurred to us to take the initiative and have the transaction reviewed for us by a qualified advisor.

We tried to explain to the IRS what solid citizens we were, that we'd just made an honest mistake, and that we really should not be penalized for this honest oversight. Lots of letters went back and forth, but the IRS held firm. We paid the bill.

It was, all told, a very expensive and upsetting process. It was also one heck of an education. Among other things, we learned that the IRS is certainly not a "user-friendly" nor "user-sensitive" organization to deal with.

Our second experience came during the settling of the estate that led to our inheritance. As we have noted, the encounter was unpleasant because the process lasted so long, it was so difficult to understand, and there were so many family members and professionals involved. Everyone's affairs were trapped in limbo for a long time. As you might guess, mistakes were made by almost everyone involved, communications got confused, professionals had differences of opinion, and nerves became frayed.

In retrospect, we can see that these problems were not fundamentally of the IRS's making, but rather stemmed from the complex nature of the estate situation we had presented it with. This too was a learning experience, and we have put into practice what we have learned in our major-gifting efforts—and in our estate planning, for that matter.

Today, we have absolutely no fear of an IRS audit, we lose no sleep over it, and our giving is in no way constrained by it. In fact, we fully expect to be audited at some point because our level of giving, in relation to our income, is likely to trigger some kind of inquiry. We have made that basic assumption in our planning.

The reason we aren't worried about any future encounter with the IRS is that we have learned to follow these four rules:

- We have an ongoing relationship with a good lawyer and a capable accountant, and we review any taxable event with one or the other, or both, before we proceed.
- We keep good records.
- We work to reduce the potential for error in every IRS-related action by avoiding the more complex and error-prone gifting techniques whenever possible.
- We avoid the more "aggressive" tax-saving methods that we know or strongly suspect are likely to trigger an IRS challenge.

Thanks to our four rules, we are at ease with our relationships with taxing bodies, and tax concerns do not hinder our participation in major gifting.

12
Special Cases

As we look at the financial side of major gifting, there are two types of investments that take on a special significance. These are (1) assets—generally stock, mutual fund shares, and property—that have appreciated significantly from the price you originally paid for them, and (2) tax-deferred retirement plans. Both types of investments have important tax implications that should be considered as part of a major-gifting effort.

Capital and Capital Gains Taxes

To give big dollars, people typically have to "dip into principal." That has a very ominous ring to it. We know that to many, the concept of parting with principal (or, as it is often described, capital) seems irresponsible. People may be comfortable giving from income, but selling or giving capital away can be quite a difficult thing to consider.

We would like to suggest that parting with principal, particularly for gifting to the charities of your choice, may actually be a fine thing to do. It can be a very tax-efficient way to give appreciated stock (or other assets), because, in essence, you get rewarded twice. First, you get the tax deduction on the appreciated market value of the asset. Second, no capital gains tax needs to be paid by you or by your receiving charity. (There are exceptions to this general rule, so please consult with your advisors.)

Some Rationalizations

We have found the following logic helpful in reaching an objective point of view on the subject of parting with capital and dealing with related capital gains taxes.

- **Pay Now or Pay Later.** The issue is not *whether* you owe the capital gains tax (you do), but *when* you pay it. If you sell an appreciated asset (typically a stock or mutual fund) this year, you pay the capital gains tax this year. If you sell the stock three years from now, you pay the capital gains tax three years from now. The only difference is that in the second case, the government lets you hold on to the owed tax amount for a while, and you can get some interest or growth from it.

   That can be a big factor if you hold the stock for many years, but it may not be such a big deal over a few years' time. In any case, if you really hate the idea of paying capital gains tax, then gift the stock. Neither you nor your charity will have to pay capital gains tax, plus you will probably be able to take a tax deduction for the full amount of the gift. Again, talk with your advisors about this one.

- **Think of it as similar to a mortgage.** Another useful way of looking at capital gains is to compare stock ownership with home ownership. When we own a home with a mortgage, most of us understand that what we actually own is the equity in the home, not the market value of the home. It is clear that in any calculation of our net worth, it is the equity that counts. And if we sell that home, the cash needed to pay off the mortgage will come off the top; we would walk away with a check for the difference—minus some fees, of course. The equity is what counts.

Stock ownership can be viewed in much the same way. If we sell the stock or mutual fund shares, we must pay the capital gains tax that has accumulated. We walk away with the difference, minus some fees. Once again, it is the "equity" that counts. Yet we are encouraged by conventional wisdom to view this tax as a penalty to be avoided, rather than as a liability to be addressed.

How to Avoid Capital Gains Taxes

Capital gains taxes can certainly be postponed, but options for avoiding capital gains taxes are very limited. We know of only three ways to avoid paying capital gains taxes:

* **Have no capital gains.** This can be achieved by limiting your investments to those that generate income but do not produce growth. This would mean having an investment portfolio without any equities and likely keeping it all in bonds. This would be rather constraining, given that even low levels of inflation will eat away at net worth over the years if your investment portfolio does not contain some growth investments. Few professional advisors would recommend this approach.

* **Hold the stock until you die.** Your heirs will inherit the stock at a price equal to its fair market value on the day of your death. In effect, no capital gains taxes will be due. (Note that this approach doesn't work if your assets have been put in certain types of annuities, trusts, or retirement plans.) This may or may not be an appealing option depending on your age, the merits of the investments, and other investment issues.

❧ **Give the appreciated stock to charity**. This option has a lot going for it.

Our Experiences

We have found, after some false starts, that gifting appreciated stock works quite well. When we began doing our major gifting, charitable organizations often voiced interest in accepting gifted stock, but many of them really couldn't handle it smoothly. We were not at all surprised that smaller local charities were not set up for it. We were very surprised to discover that some of the larger, more sophisticated organizations were not either. If your favorite charity doesn't seem comfortable with handling a stock gift transaction, help them get a system in place. You'll be doing them a big favor.

We have been regularly gifting Philip Morris stock. We find a lot of poetic justice in that.

Retirement Accounts: A Special Case

We see tax-deferred retirement plans (including regular IRAs, but not Roth IRAs) as fine tools for effective charitable gifting. As always, we advise you to check with your advisors to be sure that these techniques will work under your plan.

Reality Check

We came to realize that we didn't really own our retirement plan; the government is just letting us hang on to it for a while. When we die and our retirement plan is paid out, it will be subject to income taxes as high as 40%. In addition, our estate could be required to pay an estate tax as high as 55% on the amount in our retirement account. (Although there are some modifying deductions here, from a big-picture point of view, this is how it works out.) Bottom line, if we leave a substantial estate, as much as 40 to 90% of our retirement plan will go for taxes. Our family would get as little as 10% of our retirement plan.

This part of our education really hurt. A great deal of our personal life savings is in our retirement plan. We contributed to it faithfully for most of our adult lives, taking quiet pride in its growth to a substantial amount. When we realized that given our current situation, the bulk of it would be taxed away at our deaths, we were sorely disappointed. Kathleen and Bill must have felt we were pretty slow to grasp the hard truth on this one. We kept asking, "You mean there is no way around this?"

Well, there is one way—*give* the money away. We'll get to that in more detail in a minute. We'd like to point out that there are some rather complex techniques for keeping your retirement plan alive into the next generation and keeping it growing in a tax-sheltered situation. However, those tools did not fit our "keep it simple" and "don't push your family members into long-term business relationship" philosophies. Check with your advisors to see whether these alternative tools might be right for your own overall plan.

Going back to "giving it away," we learned that we could leave our retirement account to the charities of our choice and incur no taxes at all if Dick were to die prematurely with substantial assets remaining in his tax-deferred retirement account. No income taxes, no estate taxes, no capital gains taxes, no anything taxes.

To recap, naming a charity as beneficiary makes sense, up to the time you must begin taking significant distributions. This generally begins at age 70½. Since everyone's situation is quite different, see your lawyer and accountant at age 70 (or before you begin distributions) to determine the best policy from that point forward.

The logic of this approach is that if we are destined to give most of it away anyway, we might as well give it to charity, rather than to the taxman. Why not bequeath the account to the charity of our choice, which would then benefit from 100% of it? If your answer to that question is that you would rather leave it to your family even if much of it was taxed away in the process, you may want to confer with your advisors on this one also. You are likely to find much more tax-efficient ways to make equivalent gifts to your family. Our deferred-tax retirement accounts are therefore set up to be passed to our favorite charities should Dick die within the next few years. As he approaches age 70, we will review all this with Kathleen and Bill and determine the best arrangement to put in place for the remainder of our lives.

The Retirement Plan as a Safety Net

When we set about determining how much to give during our lifetime, we certainly had to consider the possibility of unexpected major health problems as we aged. Like most folks, we can plan and allow fairly well for living expenses, general retirement costs, and even nursing-home expenses, but really major health problems loom as a great unknown that can be a real detriment to gifting during one's lifetime. What to do?

Here is the idea. First, set up your tax-deferred retirement plan (or IRA) to be gifted at your death. This will ensure that if you die before taking significant distributions (generally in your 70s), these assets will go to your charity, rather than to taxes. While you live, these funds are still yours and are available if you need them to cover catastrophic health expenses.

By keeping our retirement plan in our possession, available to help us cope with any extraordinary expense that

might confront us, we know we will be covered. And, knowing that, we can be comfortable gifting at a higher level during our lifetimes, even to the point of reducing the size of our
estate, with attendant estate-tax savings. The retirement plan
is our safety net, allowing us the financial freedom to do
what we would like during our lifetime.

13
Gifting to Family and Friends

THE IRS GIVES NO TAX DEDUCTIONS for gifting to family and friends. In fact, beyond a certain level, the IRS taxes family gifting quite heavily. There are, however, many tools available for gifting to family and friends. Some of them are tax-efficient, and some are not. Some have very little administrative baggage; some have a lot.

Ways to Give

The list that follows includes a number of possibilities, beginning with the more basic and progressing to the more complex. By basic, we mean options that are relatively easy to administer and therefore don't require significant involvement from your professional advisors; these options also have a low risk of eliciting IRS objections. By complex, we mean that they require higher levels of administration and carry a higher risk of IRS audit and rejection; they also require a lot of lawyer and accountant time.

Certainly, some of the more "complex" options may offer tax savings or control benefits that will justify the extra expense and the hassle for your particular case. But then again, maybe not.

1. An Estate Plan

We came to realize that the most basic financial/legal "gift" that we could give to our family was an appropriate estate plan. This involved a will, a revocable living trust (not a necessity in Colorado, but we liked some of the features it afforded), and durable powers of attorney for asset and healthcare decisions.

By preparing a comprehensive estate plan, we hope to spare our family the agony of having to decide on an executor, determine the guardian for minor children (not an issue for us, but certainly an important issue for others), and decide who gets the family heirlooms. The family will not have to sort out the many other potentially troubling legal and family decisions. We will have made those decisions for our family, and who better to make them?

Another "gift" to your family is to be sure to complete all the paperwork related to medical directives that specify the degree of "heroic care" that you want used to prolong your life. These documents generally ensure that your wishes will be followed, and your family will not have to face the additional trauma and potential conflict of guessing what you would want during your final days and hours.

Taking the initiative to create an appropriate estate plan is truly a valuable "gift" to our family.

2. *Easy Ways to Give to Family and Friends*

Here are a number of very basic ways to give assets, without gift taxes, to your family and friends. The IRS welcomes (or at least tolerates) all of these techniques. The permissible levels for some of these gifting vehicles are being increased by the 1997 tax law. Our calculations in Section 3 reflect these ongoing changes.

These techniques require no special administrative framework such as formal trusts or partnerships. No significant lawyer or accountant involvement is required to use these tools (but do check anyway). As with regular tax deductions, you need to be ready to substantiate the transactions if requested to by the IRS. Good record keeping is a must. There are no ongoing annual administrative activities, and the cost of using these gifting tools is virtually nothing.

The IRS has clearly defined limits on what gifting amounts qualify for tax-favored treatment. These "easy ways" are outlined below. We see three categories of tax-protected gifting for family and friends.

Annual Exclusion Gifting. Anyone can give as much as $10,000 to any other person (family member or not) in any given year. TABLE 13-1 provides an example of how this works for an individual (or couple) giving annual gifts to two adult children, their spouses, one grandchild each, and to a friend.

Table 13-1: Family Gifting—Annual Exclusion

Recipient	From an individual	From a couple
Child #1	$10,000	$20,000
Spouse #1	$10,000	$20,000
Grandchild #1	$10,000	$20,000
Child #2	$10,000	$20,000
Spouse #2	$10,000	$20,000
Grandchild #2	$10,000	$20,000
Friend #1	$10,000	$20,000
TOTAL per year	$70,000	$140,000

Note that this is a "use it or lose it" opportunity during any one year. If you give less than $10,000 to an individual during one year, you cannot come back the next year and make use of the "unused" portion of last year's exclusion. If you gift more than the $10,000 limit to any one person during a given year, that extra amount must be deducted from your unified credit (see below) at your death, when your estate is settled.

A gift tax return may be required if one spouse gives more than the annual exclusion. See your advisors on this issue.

Obviously, there are some soft issues here, but this is a powerful, and very simple, tool for transferring wealth.

Pay School Tuition Directly. You may pay tuition for your children and grandchildren (or for other family members or friends) without incurring a tax penalty. This is over and above the annual $10,000 exclusion.

Pay Medical Expenses Directly. As with tuition, you may pay for medical expenses and health insurance for family or friends, without incurring a tax penalty. This is also over and above the annual $10,000 exclusion.

Accumulated Gifting (The Unified Credit). In addition to this "annual gifting," the IRS allows each person a substantial level of accumulated tax-free gifting to family and friends over their lifetime, or at their death. This category (somewhat obscured by legalese) is called the unified credit exemption. TABLE 13-2 shows what the allowable levels are for the next few years. The accumulated totals can be given today, at your death, or at any time and in any combination that you might choose.

Table 13-2: Family Gifting—Unified Credit Levels

Year of death	For an individual	For a couple
1998	$625,000	$1,250,000
1999	$650,000	$1,300,000
2000	$675,000	$1,350,000
2001	$675,000	$1,350,000
2002	$700,000	$1,400,000
2003	$700,000	$1,400,000
2004	$850,000	$1,700,000
2006	$1,000,000	$2,000,000
2007	*Same as the year 2006 levels, for the foreseeable future.*	

Leave the Assets From Your Tax-deferred Retirement Plan to Family and Friends. As we discussed in Chapter 12, this can be a really bad way to pass on assets to your family because these assets are taxed, at your death, both as income and as inheritance.

3. More Complicated Ways to Gift to Family and Friends

You will need a fair amount of legal and accounting advice, and you'll need to do quite a bit of research, to determine which—if any—of these tools might be appropriate to your situation. Most of them require that legal documents be created, and most of them will entail ongoing administrative expenses of some kind. Family members may have to be involved over the long term as well.

It can be difficult to quantify what the tax savings will be in relation to the expense and family stress associated with establishing and maintaining some of these tools.

Revocable Living Trust (Family or By-pass Trusts). We've classified this option, which would be part of your estate plan, as "complicated" because it requires considerable paperwork. It is, however, a fairly conventional tool, one that is well-accepted by the IRS. Its pros and cons are predictable, and its economic benefits are quantifiable.

The family or by-pass trust is not a gifting technique, per se, but it does have the effect of saving a lot of tax dollars in estate taxes at the death of the surviving spouse. In that sense, it decidedly increases the size of the "gift" that will go to family and friends.

This type of trust is set up by a couple, either through their wills or in revocable living trusts, to ensure that a certain portion of the assets of the first to die will go into a trust (with dividends and interest to the survivor, if desired) instead of becoming property of the survivor.

This may sound difficult to deal with, but in practice it is easier to do than it sounds, and the tax benefits to your family are substantial.

Separate tax accounting must be rigorously followed if you choose this option. It is decidedly not for everyone, but we would urge you to look into it if you have or expect to have a large estate (over $1,000,000 for an individual after the year 2006.) If this technique happens to be right for you, the tax savings to your estate can be substantial in relation to the costs of setting it up and maintaining it.

As a footnote, probably the most confusing and frustrating semantic issue that we have run into in our dealings with the legal profession has been its use of the term "trust." Our lawyer friends use the term in a myriad of ways, clear to them, confusing to us. The term "trust" can mean many different things, depending on the context of its use. We suggest that when you are told that an arrangement is a trust, don't feel bad if you don't know that means. Only with clarification of what type of trust it is, in layman's terms, will you stand a fair chance of knowing what the term means or implies. Kathleen has come to be very understanding about our need for continual clarification on issues like this.

Life Insurance Vehicles. For some families, life insurance options may be appropriate. See your legal, accounting, and insurance advisors to learn what's available to you.

4. Even More Complicated Ways to Gift to Family and Friends

This includes Family Limited Partnerships, Limited Liability Companies, Grantor Retained Annuity Trusts, Qualified Personal Residence Trusts, and so on. (If you had any doubt that Kathleen is maintaining a strong presence in the background for this section, let this paragraph set your mind at ease that she certainly is.)

There are a raft of tools out there that allow you to retain something for yourself, either through some form of control or some kind of economic interest, while gifting another sort of interest to your family and friends. For instance, in the Family Limited Partnership, you retain a general partnership interest (control) while gifting limited partnership interests to others. Under current law, this is considered to be an excellent way to leverage your annual exclusion and unified credit gifts because the value of the limited partnership interest can be discounted to less than the applicable proportionate share of the underlying assets.

In the case of the Qualified Personal Residence Trust, you retain the right to live in your own home for a period of time. At the end of that time, the property will be distributed to your children. The gift will be valued according to IRS tables, and *hopefully will be less* than the actual value received by the children, which achieves good leveraging of your gifting ability.

We have had personal experience with one of these tools, and have experienced the attendant expenses and strain. We are also aware of tightened IRS scrutiny of some of these devices, and of potential legislative attack. For some of you, these sophisticated tools may work well, and Kathleen tells us that such options certainly are the trend these days.

However, we've decided that they are not for us. All we can suggest is that you look carefully, ask comprehensive questions, and make your decisions based on your goals and *your* criteria. The input of advisors who are sensitive to your needs and wants is critical here.

Aggressive or Passive Approaches?

There are whole industries built upon stretching tax-deduction limits to the maximum. There are consultants, law firms, and fund-raising organizations that are delighted to help you stretch those limits. We assume that their efforts are being mirrored by legions of IRS employees looking over taxpayers' shoulders to ensure that the limits are stretched but not broken.

We think that the current emphasis on finding the most aggressive methods for optimizing how the limits on deductions can be stretched may be the wrong path for many. These techniques may well have an important place in the overall plans of those who do millions of dollars of gifting, but when you'll be donating $5,000, or $10,000, or even $100,000 per year, they may amount to overkill.

14
Gifting to Charities

THE IRS DOES NOT PENALIZE YOU for gifting to charity. You can give as much as you want, whenever you want, and you will never get an IRS tax bill. In fact, the IRS allows you a reward for gifting to charity (a tax deduction)—up to a point. Lets talk about that point.

Limits on Tax-Deductable Giving

During any single year you can give up to 50% of your adjusted gross income (AGI) to qualified charities and be allowed an income tax deduction for the amount given. This total of 50% can be made up of as much as 30% in appreciated assets, with the remaining portion (or 20%) made up of cash or in-kind property. As you become a major donor, you will likely bump into these limitations. As you can see, they come into play if you give in the range of one-half of your income or more. This income tax deduction cut-off point is a little-publicized but important milestone. *Some charity situations may not qualify. Do see your tax advisor.*

If you give an amount of appreciated stock or mutual funds equal to more than the 30% of your AGI, you will not get an income tax deduction on this overage, but you will avoid the additional capital gains tax on this stock gift. *There is no limit to the amount of appreciated asset capital-gains tax avoidance that you and your charity can enjoy.* We find that this point is not well publicized.

Please remember that gain from the sale of capital (capital gains), withdrawals from your qualified retirement plans, and regular income are all added up to determine your AGI. For the investor who has significant capital gains activity (sells a lot of appreciated stock or mutual fund shares) this produces a higher AGI (and maximum tax-deductible limitation) than they would get from just their *regular income.*

For the really, really major donor, these factors will likely motivate some complex lawyer/accountant involvement. You can see signs of this when you run into an article about a multimillion-dollar gift donated by a well-known celebrity. Somewhere in the small print, buried deep in the article, it may be pointed out that this will be given over many years, that it will come from their family foundation, that it will be part of a charitable remainder trust, or some other indication that they didn't just take out the check book and write a check. This is a sign of tax attorneys at work in the background, making sure that the tax deductibility is as effective as possible.

For the less dramatic major-gifting level, more within the focus of this book, these limits on deduction levels have a somewhat different implication. First, the level of the proposed gift, while generous, may not justify bringing in the big guns. In other words, a reasonable cost/benefit calculation may indicate that if the potential tax savings does not justify getting into the major legal/accounting complexity that the multimillion-dollar gift most certainly does.

Second, it may remind you to be cautious in your enthusiasm for the one-time really big gift to a capital fund drive. Your fund-raising friend may suggest that if you make that large gift now, you will be able to take the related gift tax deduction over the next few years. True, but you may want to give to some other charities next year and the year after and still be able to take a tax deduction on those future gifts. Do you want to use up all your qualified gifting tax deductions this year and be unable to get deductions in the years ahead?

But these questions, while important, are really secondary in comparison to what we feel is the most important issue in these tax-deductibility discussions. And that is, *do you really want your gifting decisions to be driven by the tax deductibility-issue at all?* If you are considering a cause that you believe in and you have the funds to give, do you really want your decision to be made by the writers of the tax code, rather than by your own sense of what is the right thing to do?

At the risk of sounding contradictory—saying that deductions are important and then implying they are not—let us clarify. What we are saying is that we suggest that your quest to do what you feel is the right thing, according to your personal definition of what the right thing is, should be the driver in your charitable gifting. Follow up by doing this gifting in the most tax-efficient way that you can—not the other way around.

Getting back to the big picture on all of this, we have found that by using the straightforward tax-saving techniques, by giving steadily year after year to ensure that each year's deductibility allowances are used, and by giving appreciated assets, significant tax savings can be achieved. At the same time, we find that this tax-saving process does not intrude on the sense of reward we get in supporting causes that we care about.

Yes, we would encourage you to go ahead and give that major gift to the capital campaign for the charity you were approached to support. If you end up giving in excess of the income tax deductibility limits for that year, so be it. The cause needs your funds, you can afford it, and you will probably sleep very well that night.

Ways to Give to Charity: The Tool Chart

There are a number of IRS-approved tools and techniques available to you for optimizing your tax deductions. Selecting appropriate choices from the list can be quite a challenge. After a number of false starts, we settled on the tool chart in TABLE 14-1 as our core document for analyzing gifting tool options and making selections appropriate to your individual situation. The left column in TABLE 14-1 shows seven categories of gifting tools, ordered roughly from simplest to more complex; the top row offers fourteen criteria for evaluating each financial tool.

Categories of Gifting

1. **Simple Giving.** This is where you just drop the money in the pot, send a check, give old clothes to the Salvation Army, or attend a fund-raising event. This is the everyday stuff, not donations that have necessarily been planned or organized in any way. If you keep accurate records, you can take a deduction for these gifts on your income tax return. In general, we are not talking about really big gifts here. We're talking about a range of a few dollars up to $1,000 or so.

2. **Giving Appreciated Assets.** This category includes gifting some of the appreciated stock and mutual fund shares you have collected over the years, as well as some other types of appreciated property, including real estate. Look again at Chapter 12 for more on this subject and related capital gains tax factors.

3. **Give Your Tax-deferred Retirement Plan or Regular IRA (not Roth) at Your Death.** For those with substantial estates, the income tax and estate tax burden to your family can be in the 40 to 90% category. Naming a charity as

Table 14-1: The Tool Chart.

Charitable Gifting—Tools and Techniques Listed by Increasing Complexity

	1 DONOR INVOLVEMENT	2 TAX SAVINGS	3 LEGAL FEES ONE TIME	4 LEGAL FEES ON-GOING	5 ONE TIME	6 ON-GOING	7 IRS INVOLVEMENT ONGOING	8 EASE OF ANALYSIS	DONOR'S CONTROL BEFORE DEATH			DONOR'S CONTROL AFTER DEATH		
									9 ASSET OWNERSHIP	10 ASSET INVESTMENT POLICY	11 DISTRIBUTION POLICY	12 ASSET OWNERSHIP	13 ASSET INVESTMENT POLICY	14 DISTRIBUTION POLICY
1 SIMPLE GIFTING CASH, CHECKS, IN-KIND, EVENTS	VERY LOW	- REGULAR DEDUCTION	NONE	NONE	NONE	NONE	NONE	EASY	NONE	NONE	TOTAL	N/A	N/A	N/A
2 GIVE APPRECIATED ASSETS TYPICALLY STOCK OR MUTUAL FUNDS	LOW	- REGULAR DEDUCTION - CAP GAINS TAXES	NONE	NONE	LOW	NONE	NONE	EASY	NONE	NONE	TOTAL	N/A	N/A	N/A
3 BEQUEST RETIREMENT PLAN / IRA AT DEATH	LOW	40% TO 90% OF THE TOTAL ACCT	LOW	NONE	NONE	NONE	NONE	EASY	TOTAL	TOTAL	N/A	NONE	NONE	DONOR'S CHOICE
4 BEQUEST ESTATE AT DEATH	LOW	ALL TAXES	LOW	NONE	NONE	NONE	NONE	EASY	TOTAL	TOTAL	N/A	NONE	NONE	DONOR'S CHOICE
5 GIVE TO A COMMUNITY FOUNDATION	MEDIUM	- REGULAR DEDUCTION - CAP GAINS TAXES	LOW	NONE	LOW	MEDIUM	HIGH	FAIRLY EASY	NONE	NONE	DONOR MAY ADVISE	NONE	NONE	DONOR MAY ADVISE
6 "PLANNED GIFTING" GIFTING TRUSTS AND ANNUTIES	HIGH	- REGULAR DEDUCTION - CAP GAINS TAXES	HIGH	NONE	HIGH	VERY HIGH	HIGH	COMPLEX TO VERY COMPLEX	NONE	NONE	VARIES	NONE	NONE	VARIES
7 SET UP A PRIVATE FOUNDATION	VERY HIGH	- REGULAR DEDUCTION - CAP GAINS TAXES	VERY HIGH	HIGH	VERY HIGH	VERY HIGH	VERY HIGH	COMPLEX TO VERY COMPLEX	CONTROL IS RETAINED BY DONOR'S TRUSTEES			CONTROL IS RETAINED BY DONOR'S TRUSTEES		

beneficiary is a straightforward method of moving these assets to your charities rather than to the government. See Chapter 12 for more on this.

4. Bequest Your Remaining Assets (Other than Retirement Plans) at Your Death. This means you just hang on to your estate and name specified charities to receive it at your death. In this case no taxes of any kind will be due when you die.

5. Give to a Community Foundation. Many communities have foundations set up to accept donated assets and systematically manage and distribute these assets for you. You can generally retain the right to advise on which charities receive the income from your donated assets.

6. Do "Planned Gifting." In this process, you turn assets over to an established charity or a trust, during your lifetime, retaining certain benefits for yourself or for other specified individuals.

7. Set Up a Private Foundation. When you create a private foundation, you transfer assets into your own foundation. You (or whoever you specify) retain control of the management and distribution of the foundation assets into perpetuity.

Each of these techniques has its own merits and demerits, depending upon an individual's specific circumstances. An individual or a family might choose a combination of tools, or perhaps vary their choices as their ages and circumstances change.

Evaluation Criteria

Let's examine the fourteen evaluation criteria presented in TABLE 14-1 in a bit more detail.

1. Donor Involvement. Some donors may wish to give without having to deal with fund-raisers, lawyers, accountants, or the IRS. Others may want to be involved in the process—or at least won't find such involvement to be a drawback. Still others may feel that involvement with advisors and the IRS is a reasonable price to pay for the level of control they wish to retain.

2. Tax Savings. As we've said before, tax savings are certainly a major factor in serious charitable giving. You should note that the degree of tax savings does not fundamentally increase as you move down the chart. However, the degree of control retained by the donor generally increases as you move into the more complex gifting arrangements.

3 and 4. Legal Fees. There is a real difference between the fees involved in setting up a gifting device and the fees involved in maintaining that device. For example, some of the more complex tools may require periodic legal review and modification in light of tax law changes. Likewise, on the accounting side, some of the more complex options may require the filing of annual tax returns.

5 and 6. Accounting Fees. The issues given for items 3 and 4 apply here as well.

7. Ongoing IRS Involvement. By this we mean the ongoing, annual need for the preparation of tax returns and the review of changes in tax law that may affect arrangements that have been put in place. Some people are uncomfortable dealing with lawyers, accountants, and the IRS, and prefer to avoid that kind of contact as much as possible. Others either don't mind or may even find such involvement challenging and interesting.

You can usually avoid ongoing involvement with professional advisors and the IRS if you choose the simplest tools for tax-efficient gifting. If, however, you choose gifting tools that allow you to retain a substantial level of control, ongoing contact with your advisors and the IRS is generally going to be required.

8. Ease of Analysis. We feel that being able to quantify the cost of administering a given technique and the true tax savings achieved is very important to the tool selection process, particularly when considered in context with the other elements of your estate situation. It can be very difficult to determine the true costs and tax savings that come with using the more complex techniques. As you move down the list of options, the difficulty of ascertaining how cost-effective the technique is tends to increase significantly.

9 through 14. Control. Control is important to everyone at one level or another. We have found that control of our overall time involvement is important to us. Some people care most about retaining control of the management and distribution of their assets. Others are comfortable in turning that type of control over to others—in fact, they may be eager to relinquish control and free themselves from that kind of involvement.

Myths and Conventional Wisdom of Charitable Gifting

There are some basics that "everybody knows" (or at least that everyone thinks they know) that we had to put in perspective before we were able to reach any conclusions about which gifting techniques were right for us. Let's examine a few of these popular myths about gifting.

Myth 1: Tax deductibility is the driver. It's easy to fall into the trap of thinking that the limit of tax deductibility is also the limit of what you can give. It isn't. You can give away as much as you want to charity, whenever you want. The government doesn't care. It won't charge a penalty for your giving. When it comes to gifting to family and friends, the government does care, and over a given amount, it will penalize you (with a tax, that is.)

We have to remind ourselves all the time that we should not be limited in our thinking by the issue of tax deductibility—we need only be guided by it. That said, we have found that with the judicious use of the more straightforward gifting approaches, we have been pretty much able to give what we could afford and still manage to stay within the tax-deductible limits.

Myth 2: If the technique is more complex, it must be saving more taxes. Hardly. Nowhere is it written that increased complexity correlates with effectiveness. On the contrary, it is quite possible (perhaps even probable) that more-complex gifting arrangements, with their higher legal and accounting costs, may be less financially effective in the long run. The likely cutoff point is related to the size of the donation. The higher cost may be reasonable for a really large donation, but for a smaller one, the extra expenses can rapidly eat into the tax savings you are seeking.

Myth 3: If you "plan your gifting," you should be drawn to "planned gifting." The term "Planned Gifting" is fund-raiser shorthand for a particular group of gifting techniques. They are usually referring to the use of trusts or other long-term financial arrangements for transferring assets. Examples of these tools are Charitable Remainder Trusts, Charitable Lead Trusts, and Gifting Annuities. When members of the nonprofit world focus on major gifting, they generally talk a lot about such "Planned Gifting."

This terminology can inadvertently imply that if you "plan" your gifting, Planned Gifting tools are automatically the way to go about it. That's a big leap, and it's not necessarily the case. We found that we can have a fine long-term gifting plan that does not include any of the Planned Gifting tools recommended by the fund-raising industry. We may someday make use of one of these tools, but they are not right for us now.

Myth 4: You can make good major-gifting decisions independent of your total estate and net-worth situation. When you do major gifting and want to get the related tax breaks, it is really important to integrate the choices you make with the rest of your estate plan. Your chosen charity may be happy to provide suggestions and even legal and accounting advice, but it is unlikely to be in a position to advise you comprehensively on the best tool for you to use, given your overall situation.

Unless, of course, you want to inform them of your total financial situation (including your income, net worth, and other gifting activities, for starters) and your total family situation (including any potential family frictions that might be lurking below the surface). Most of us would not choose to share that kind of information beyond the circle of our own professional advisors.

By all means go ahead and learn about the range of gifting options that your charity has to offer, but then we recommend that you take the information to your own advisors to get a review of the choices that seem to best suit your situation. We are not suggesting that charities and their advisors would try to mislead you; their financial and legal specialists are most likely fully qualified to offer expert advice on tax-related gifting issues. Rather, we recommend consulting with your own chosen advisors to ensure that your final gifting decisions will be guided by professionals who have a full understanding of the details of your overall financial and personal situation.

Endowment Giving

Giving to a charity's endowment fund is a gifting technique that may or may not be attractive depending on the amount of *control* over the assets that the donor would like to retain or give up. The tax implications of endowment giving are roughly the same as gifting for direct annual usage.

Current Versus Future Usage

As a donor, you can choose to give to a charity with the understanding that the funds will be spent fairly soon—within a year in most cases. We think of this as "current usage." You might also give to a charity knowing that it will hold the assets for the long term, investing them for growth and income, and making annual distributions to be spent during that specific year. This is an endowment fund.

When we started gifting, we decided to give annually for current usage, retaining the rest of our assets and managing the investment and distribution of those funds ourselves. We wanted to retain control of our assets, and we wanted to make the gifting decisions. As time went on, we began to appreciate some of the gray areas. The benefits of a number of endowment options became clearer to us. We discovered that there were a number of ways in which giving money in the form of an endowment would be advantageous to our charities and to ourselves.

Endowment Opportunities

We found a number of specific endowment options that began to look quite appealing to us. We have already or will be giving serious consideration to these methods.

- **Bequest a retirement plan.** In Chapter 12 we
  discussed the merits of making a bequest of a tax-

deferred retirement plan. Choosing an endowment fund managed by an organization that we respect looks like a good way to ensure that these assets will be well-managed for the long term.

* **Establish a family tradition of philanthropy.** Gifting money to an endowment fund and designating a member (or members) of our family as the fund advisor(s) to advise on distribution of income and capital will help establish a tradition of philanthropy for the family.

* **Delegate asset and distribution management.** For the long-term donor, a time might come when the burdens of managing annual distributions to charities would become too much to handle. Giving to an endowment fund where the nonprofit organization assumes responsibility for managing the assets and making good distribution decisions could be a useful option.

* **Bequest to changing nonprofits.** We would like to bequest money, after our deaths, to some of the organizations we currently support. But what would happen if the mission, governance, and effectiveness of these organizations changed over the years, until they no longer met the criteria that we had established? We are therefore considering the bequest of some funds to an endowment that would have the power to shift these funds, as appropriate, ensuring that the distribution would be in line with our original intentions.

* **Honor a relative or friend.** Giving to an endowment in the name of an admired relative or friend is an excellent way to honor their memory.

Trust and Confidence

As you can see, giving to an endowment has much to do with the degree of control that you are willing to give up, and the level of trust and confidence that you have in the organization you turn the funds over to.

For us, having confidence in a charity's long-term ability to manage money, to make good distribution decisions (based on current conditions), and to maintain organizational stability are the key to being comfortable with shifting assets to an endowment fund. We expect that would be the case for many people.

"Long term" is the key phrase. You can give an annual donation to almost any charity and be fairly sure (with a little bit of effort) that the gift will go to the effort you intended and be used sensibly. With an endowment, however, you are projecting into the future. ("In perpetuity" is a common phrase in these agreements.) People you don't even know will be making decisions about issues you may not even be currently aware of.

If you are drawn to the endowment option, you may choose to work with an organization such as a Community Foundation, your favorite hospital, your alma mater, or another organization that meets your criteria for long-range trust.

15
Our Gifting Tool Choices

THIS CHAPTER CERTAINLY REFLECTS the "personal" side of major gifting. Let's look at the process we went through and the choices that we wound up with.

The Process

It looks so simple in retrospect, but what a process the selection business turned out to be for us. We would like to tell you that if we had to do it all over, it would be a short, efficient process. But we think not.

First of all, selecting the right tools is ultimately a process of self-examination—one that requires a determination to follow through. We realized that we needed to figure out what we wanted to accomplish and what was important to us before settling on the methods that would best help us accomplish those goals.

By now, it should be clear that we used tax implications as just one of the factors in our decision process, not as the only factor. Once we had decided what we wanted to accomplish and had a fair understanding of the tool choices available to us, the final selections were relatively easy to identify.

We have come to know ourselves better as a result of going through this process. We've probably always been the way we are, but now we see ourselves more clearly. Some of the things we have come to realize about ourselves have had a direct impact our on choice of gifting tools. For example, we like closure. We like to have issues laid to rest. We like to think things out, ponder the alternatives, reach the best conclusions that we can, and then let it be. We like the policy of

"Do it once, do it right, and get on with your life." We are comfortable with a periodic review of the plans we've put in place, and we acknowledge the need to make appropriate midcourse corrections as necessary.

These characteristics have greatly affected our relationships with our professional advisors. We like to have significant involvement with our advisors at the start of the process and less involvement with them on an ongoing basis. Obviously, the advisors we work best with are those who share (or at least can comfortably accommodate) these views.

And when it came to choosing our gifting tools, we realized that these factors in our nature would be crucial. Our tool choices reflect our ages, our interests, our family relationships, our level of wealth, and our sense of appropriate control. Although the basics and the rules may be generic, translating them into a plan for an individual or a family is very personal indeed.

Our Choices

After all the soul-searching, evaluating, and testing, here's what we've found works well for us.

Simple Gifting: Cash, Checks, In-kind Donations, and Events. We do some of this. We do participate in some impulse giving, dropping a few bucks in the pot, buying the raffle tickets, or sending a check to a cause that catches our interest. We do our charities and ourselves a favor by donating in-kind items we no longer have need for. We go to the events that tend to inform and entertain but don't go to many where the priority is the other way around.

Give Appreciated Assets. This is currently our primary tool. It works with our investment arrangements quite nicely. We gain the regular tax deduction plus the benefit of avoiding capital gains tax. The process is easy for us, for our charities, for our investment advisors, and for our accountant at tax time.

Bequest Retirement Plan at Death. As we have noted, we have arranged things so that if Dick should die prematurely, his retirement plan assets will go to the Community Foundation for management and distribution to charities in the health and human services areas. We are pleased to know that these assets would go to local social service needs rather than to the government's general fund.

Bequest Estate at Death. It is our plan to minimize the value of our estate and related estate taxes by distributing assets during our lifetime. Therefore, we don't expect bequests (other than the bequest of our retirement plan) to be a major factor in our eventual estate settlement, although we do expect to include some miscellaneous smaller bequests.

Give to a Community Foundation. Community Foundations offer a number of donor-oriented ways to handle gifted assets. As noted in Chapter 14, there are a number of methods of endowment giving that might meet your needs, and Community Foundations are well-equipped to provide endowment-related services. In our experience, the Community Foundation has been able to help us meet a number of our gifting goals.

"Planned Gifting." As yet, we have not found that Planned Gifting tools have any benefits that truly apply to us. Maybe someday these options will be useful for us, but not now.

Set Up a Private Foundation. We gave thought to this early in our research period. At that time we shied away from a private foundation because we were determined to keep things simple. We also didn't have a good understanding of the full array of gifting tools. Looking back, we realize that our instinctive choice was a good one for us.

Our estate, although comfortable, is probably not big enough to justify the overhead that comes with creating a private foundation, and given our priorities for minimizing administrative duties, we really would not want to have to be involved at the level a personal foundation would require. Given the diverse nature of our next-generation family, it does not look like it would be beneficial to require them to work together as trustees. Therefore, we're comfortable with the decision that a private foundation is not for us, but we readily acknowledge that it may be right for many.

THE
FINANCIAL
SIDE

16
The Brown Family

IN SECTION 1, WE COVERED the personal side of major gifting. In Section 2, we discussed the technicalities of tax-efficient gifting. In this section, we will cover financial analysis of major gifting in the context of a lifetime net-worth budget. Before we start our in-depth look at financial analysis, we'd like to introduce you to the Brown family, one of six mythical families that will help us explain the process.

Our guess is that most readers would like an overview of where this whole discussion is going before they get into the chapters that follow. Therefore, we are going to jump ahead and give you an overview of the Brown family's situation as an example of what we'll be doing in remaining chapters of the book.

We've chosen to begin with the Browns because we wanted your first look at the summary data to be an attention-getting one. The Browns qualify as "very comfortable," with a starting net worth of $2.5 million.

Starting Data

Both Mr. and Mrs. Brown will be 60 years old on January 1, 2000, and they will both live to be 90 years old. Their financial situation at the beginning of our analysis is shown in TABLE 16-1. They have $800,000 in regular investments, $700,000 in their deferred retirement plans, and $300,000 equity in their home. They also have a $700,000 life insurance policy (face value). These items create their total net worth of $2,500,000. We use the face value of the insurance policy as part of the net worth of an individual or couple, rather than the cash value. We do this to avoid the programming complication that would be introduced by working with the varying "cash value" of an insurance policy. Typically, the full "face value" would become available only at the death of the policyholder. We suggest you to keep this insurance factor in mind, particularly as you look at your consideration of how much is "enough." Please confer with your advisors on your specific insurance situation.

Table 16-1: The Brown Family Starting Data

Starting year	2000
Age at start	60
Age at death	90
Net worth	
Regular investments	800,000
Retirement accounts	700,000
Real estate equity	300,000
Life insurance	700,000
Total net worth	$2,500,000
Annual gifting	
Family	20,000
Charity	28,000
Total annual gifting	$48,000
Annual living expenses	$90,000
Anticipated inheritance	$500,000
"Enough"	$2,000,000

Reference: Appendix Table A-2

Net-Worth Categories. You will note that we look at net worth somewhat differently than the typical net-worth listings you may see in the popular financial magazines or even on your bank's mortgage and loan application forms. Because this type of analysis can become very complicated, we have worked hard to keep the number of asset categories to the minimum required. Our criteria for selecting these categories was to group assets by how they are treated from a tax point of view and by what level of total return might be realized.

We have not included personal property, such as cars, computers, furniture, boats, jewelry, or artwork. They are certainly assets, but they tend to depreciate as the years go by, unlike other investments. Unless you are a serious collector, these kinds of assets usually don't have great impact on the strategy issues that we are addressing. Also, these items are generally possessions that are changed or replaced over time and any analysis that included them would likely be obsolete within a couple of years or even sooner.

That said, it is good to remember that personal possessions have some interesting aspects to consider when you are quantifying your estate plan. As noted, personal possessions typically do not contribute to your real availability of funds. You generally do not sell your cars, furniture, or jewelry to cover a cash shortfall during a given year. Yet these same items do become part of your taxable net worth at your death. So, if you are uneasy with leaving personal possessions out of your calculations, consider the following approach.

Assume that you have a certain amount of value in personal possessions—say, around $150,000. Half of the total is in items that might increase in value with the rate of inflation, and the other half might hold value but that value is unlikely to go up over time. To recognize these values, you can add $75,000 to the "equity" net-worth category (which is programmed to grow with inflation) and $75,000 to the "insurance" category (which is not programmed to grow in value). This shortcut recognizes the financial impact of personal possessions without adding complication to the program.

Anticipated Inheritance. Some would say that including an anticipated inheritance in an analysis of this type is unwise or unseemly. On the contrary, we feel that since the aim here is to determine the best way to manage your lifetime estate situation in view of your goals for major gifting and reducing tax payments, it is necessary to consider all sources in your planning. For one thing, you might conclude that your estate is big enough already, and you could "disclaim" the inheritance and let it go directly to your children or grandchildren, thus skipping one or two generations of inheritance taxes. (Now that is really a tax-optimized family gift!) To do comprehensive tax planning, you need to consider any significant inheritance as part of the big picture.

What Is "Enough"? This is the baseline net worth of which we have spoken. It is the amount that the Browns do not want to allow their net worth to drop below. They feel that if they maintain a total estate value of at least $2,000,000 (increasing by inflation as the years go by), that will be "enough" to meet their comfort-zone asset requirements.

As TABLE 16-1 shows, the Browns will be spending $90,000 on living expenses (apart from taxes) during the year 2000. They plan to gift $20,000 to family and $28,000 to charity that year, and they anticipate increasing these amounts as appropriate over their lifetimes. The Browns also estimate that they will be receiving an inheritance of $500,000 in the year 2007.

The Browns are equity investors, in for the long haul. They enjoy a comfortable lifestyle, but spend less than their combined income and portfolio growth, so their estate is increasing as each year goes by.

Gifting Options. The Browns are considering two gifting options in their long-term planning. First, they will consider doing no annual gifting to charity and family. Under this option, they would not bequest their qualified retirement plans to charity. Their second gifting option is to do significant annual gifting to family and friends, as well as to charity, during their lifetimes. Under this option they would plan on bequesting their retirement plans to charity.

Note that the Browns (and all the other families that we include in our samples) are following a gifting strategy that calls for roughly a 50–50 split between family gifting and charitable gifting. Obviously, you may chose this middle ground strategy or you may choose some other balance between family and charity gifting.

Lifetime Summary Data

TABLE 16-2, on the next page, summarizes where the Brown's money will go during their lifetimes under the two gifting options. Think of it as a financial score card, one that delivers what is truly the core of the financial message of this book. The table shows what happens *with* and *without* gifting. Additional figures and tables will show this summary data in more detail.

Take a few minutes to compare the numbers. They say a lot about what can be accomplished by steady, lifetime giving, using simple tools. Note especially that the Browns are able to give $3,400,000 to charity during their lifetimes using this approach. Note also that they will pay almost $6,000,000 less in taxes using the *with* gifting option. This massive difference is largely due to the fact that under the *with* gifting option, the Brown's estate did not grow so large that it was significantly impacted by the 55% estate tax rate.

A few words about the Alternative Minimum Tax (AMT). If you have not as yet run into this tax, you will likely encounter it soon. It is an override calculation that can come into play when a taxpayer has a relatively high income with

Table 16-2: The Brown Family Summary Data

	With gifting	Without gifting
Net worth		
Starting	$ 2,500,000	$ 2,500,000
Ending	4,800,000	10,400,000
"Enough"		
Starting	2,000,000	2,000,000
Ending	3,600,000	3,600,000
Total lifetime gifting		
Taxes	2,700,000	8,700,000
Charity	3,400,000	0
Family	3,500,000	5,400,000
Total lifetime gifting	**9,600,0000**	**14,100,000**
Total lifetime taxes		
Income	1,800,000	2,900,000
Capital Gains	350,000	800,000
Estate	600,000	5,000,000
Total taxes	**2,750,000**	**8,700,000**

Reference: Appendix Table B-2, Table C-2, Figure D-2, Table E-2

high deductions, which results in an income-tax calculation that is relatively low. The AMT figure is produced by a re-calculation of the tax return, and the taxpayer must pay whichever amount is the highest—the basic tax calculation or the AMT. Because this calculation is way too complex to get into here, we do not include it in our examples. But do keep this qualifier in mind. To the best of our knowledge, the AMT is not a decisive factor in the conclusions we present, but it is likely to somewhat reduce the income-tax savings that we have calculated.

This analysis is based on the IRS regulations that were in effect in 1999. Things will no doubt have changed by the time you read this. Inheritance tax rates may have been modified. Perhaps the capital gains tax regulations will have been changed, or maybe the regulations on annual family gifting will have been modified. Nonetheless, we think the concepts represented by these charts are likely to remain valid, barring a radical change to the whole tax code. In any case, please do keep in touch with your advisors.

Figure 16-1: Net Worth for the Brown Family

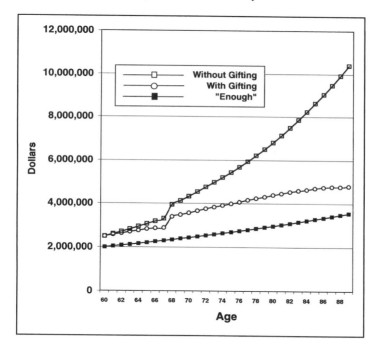

Brown Family Net Worth

	Starting year	Ending year
Without gifting	$ 2,500,000	$ 10,393,275
With gifting	2,500,000	4,794,037
"Enough"	2,000,000	3,551,689

Figure 16-2: Total Gifting for the Brown Family

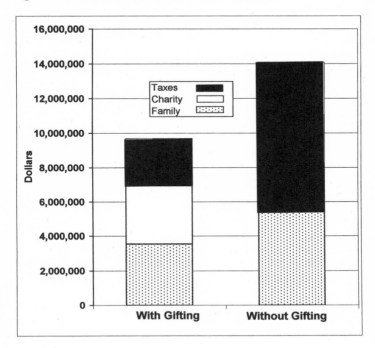

Brown Family Lifetime Gifting

	With gifting	Without gifting
Taxes	$ 2,747,788	$ 8,662,377
Charity	3,383,465	0
Family	3,545,610	5,413,303
Totals	9,676,863	14,075,681

Lifetime Summary: Two Graphs and a Chart

We have prepared two additional detailed summary graphs (with data tables) and another detailed table to give you a more extensive view of the 30-year results of the Brown family's financial choices.

Net Worth. FIGURE 16-1 shows how the Brown's net worth changes during their lifetime, for both the *with* gifting and *without* gifting options, in relation to the level of net worth that they consider to be "enough." Note that the upper line shows how their net worth would soar *without* gifting as they grow older—well beyond the level that they consider "enough" to meet their needs. (Ah, the power of compound interest, sound investing, and prudent spending.) On the *with* gifting track, their net worth remains well above their projected "enough" level while letting them participate in the distribution of their wealth during their lifetimes.

Total Distribution of Assets. FIGURE 16-2 is a graph that shows the accumulated amount that the Browns would "give" to taxes, charity, and family during their lifetimes, *with* and *without* doing major gifting along the way. With gifting, their taxes go way down, donations to charity go way up, and family gifting apparently drops considerably. (More on that "apparently" comment a bit later.)

The Detail Summary. TABLE 16-3 (two parts) shows some of the background behind the summaries that you have just reviewed. The table highlights a number of the significant con-

Table 16-3: The Brown Family Total Gifting—Detail Summary

	With Gifting		Without Gifting		Difference
	Amount	%	Amount	%	
Taxes					
Income Taxes					
Retirement Plans	1,169,736		1,492,078		322,341
Other	595,965		1,387,328		791,363
Income Taxes - Total	1,765,701		2,879,406		1,113,704
Capital Gains Taxes	354,640		803,000		448,360
Estate Taxes	627,447		4,979,972		4,352,525
Total Taxes	2,747,788	28.4%	8,662,377	61.5%	5,914,589
Charity					
Annual	1,570,378		0		-1,570,378
At Death	1,813,087 *		0		-1,813,087
Total Charity	3,383,465	35.0%	0	0.0%	-3,383,465
Family					
Annual	1,121,699		0		-1,121,699
At Death	2,423,911		5,413,303 AY443		2,989,392
Total Family	3,545,610	36.6%	5,413,303	38.5%	1,867,693
Total Gifting	9,676,863	100.0%	14,075,681	100.0%	4,398,817

* From undistributed retirement plans.

Table 16-3: The Brown Family Total Gifting—Highlights

With Gifting, the Brown Family's			
Estate is reduced by:		5,599,238	
Income taxes are reduced by		1,113,704	
Capital Gains taxes are reduced by		448,360	
Estate taxes are reduced by		4,352,525	
Total taxes are reduced by		5,914,589	
Charities receive an average of	52,346	1,570,378	during Brown's lifetime, plus
	per year, or	1,813,087	at their death
for a total lifetime charity gifting of		3,383,465	
Family receives an average of	37,390	1,121,699	during Brown's lifetime, plus
	per year, or	2,423,911	at their death
for a total lifetime family gifting of		3,545,610	
In Addition:			
If the family members invest their annual gifting of		1,121,699	as they get it each year,
it will grow to		3,155,480	
and this, added to the		2,423,911	given at their death
will add up to a total lifetime family gifting of		5,579,392	
which compares with the		5,413,303	given at their death
that they would have received with the "without giving" scenario.			

clusions indicated by this analysis. Please do take the time to study it in some detail. It says a great deal about the general relationships between the *with* and *without* gifting strategies.

You will likely find the table to be self-explanatory, so we won't dwell on a long explanation. We do, however, want to point out and emphasize a couple of insights that may not be so obvious.

First, note that the largest portion of the total *with* gifting tax bill consists of income tax on their qualified retirement plans. This is because the Browns lived to an age where a good share of their retirement plan assets had been distributed to them, and they had been required to pay roughly 40% of these assets as income taxes. We are assuming these major distributions, plus their other income, will put them into the maximum tax bracket at this point. The frustrating part of this is that if they died at, say, 75 years old, before a major portion of these assets were distributed from their retirement accounts, they could have bequested the accounts to charity and no taxes would have been paid.

Sad to say, it does appear that the only way for the Browns or any other similarly well-to-do couple to avoid a roughly 40% income-tax bite on their qualified retirement account assets is to have died before their time. Not a real good tax-savings strategy. We are told that Congress is considering allowing gifts of qualified retirement assets to receive some form of tax relief. If this happens, it would be a very important factor to consider in your charitable gift planning.

The other very significant issue that is worthy of detailed consideration has to do with the amount that is left to family under the two gifting options. Note that the total amount given to charity and family in the *with* gifting option is roughly the same as the amount given just to family under the *without* gifting option. This makes sense since it is the Brown's strategy to have a roughly 50–50 distribution of gifts to family and charity.

The big implication here is that in the *with* gifting option, a good share of the gifting comes to the family (and to the charities) *during the Brown's lifetimes*—rather than at their deaths—a practice that both the family members and the charities would probably look upon favorably.

The Family Situation

Our accounting friends call the dollar side of this giving during the Brown's lifetime (versus holding and investing the money for the net 30 years) "net present value," and they can calculate these numbers with great accuracy. For the purpose of our discussion, we can be satisfied with our basic common-sense knowledge, which tells us that a dollar placed in a recipient's hands today is worth a lot more to them than a dollar received 30 years from now. The more personal side of this is the relative value of the funds to family and friends for such immediate needs as tuition, down-payments on a home, coping with major illnesses, and so on, versus an inheritance they might receive 30 years later.

While the charities' needs are different, their desire to see some of the money on a regular basis over the next 30 years, rather than waiting for 30 years to get a (granted) much larger amount, is readily understandable. On the charity side, this need for ongoing giving is perhaps even more dramatic than with the family examples, since so many of the needs of charities are very immediate. For example, if you are supporting food banks, homeless shelters, disaster relief, and the like, the needs are now. If your charitable inclination is toward the environment, perhaps saving open space, for example, the open space you would hope to protect is probably going to be well beyond protection 30 years from now.

Another powerful consideration in the timing of your family gifting is the economics of shifting assets from your estate to your children's estates, on a regular basis, during your lifetime. If you gift on an annual basis, you can shift a lot of money, tax free. This saves a lot of estate taxes; since these gifted assets will have already been transferred, no estate tax will be pending on these transferred assets at your death. But every bit as important is the fact that if your children invest these gifted assets (rather then spending them), the growth will be in their estate, so upon your death no estate taxes will be due on the growth, either. The "In Addition" calculation in TABLE 16-3 quantifies this factor.

Assuming that your family is willing to invest for the future, rather that spend on current needs and wants, this annual family gifting, with investment, is a terrific way to make generational transfers of wealth.

This issue of transferring assets to family certainly reminds us of some of the important soft issues. In many cases, those of us transferring assets to our adult children on a regular annual basis might like to see some of the transferred assets being used to enhance their lifestyles—that is, used for immediate spending. But we probably hope that the bulk of these gifted assets will go into their estates, to be invested for their retirement and perhaps for their children's benefit. In some cases, we might worry that transferring assets to our adult children without any strings attached might not be a good thing to do. Depending on the individual situation, it might even be a very bad thing to do.

If you are uneasy about transferring assets to family members during your lifetime, but you still want to take advantage of tax-efficient gifting to their estates, you may want to consider using a Crummey Trust (the name of a specific type of gifting trust, not an editorial observation). Or you could look at gifting to a trust using part of your total Unified Credit exemption. Your estate attorney will be able to supply some recommendations for you here.

This is one of those classic examples of when strictly applied financial principles would identify the ongoing transfer of assets, using the $10,000 per year gifting allowance, as a good thing to do, but family issues may dictate that it would not, after all, be such a good thing to do. Clearly, the tax advantages need to be weighed against the other issues in order to arrive at a decision that is right for the specific situation.

As you can see, given the assumptions we've made, the Browns are in a great position to give a lot of money to charity during their lifetimes, without penalizing their chosen lifestyle, and while using some good options for transferring assets to their families. And, they can do the gifting they want while retaining a substantial asset buffer to ensure that they will have "enough" during their lifetimes.

17
The Family Financial Program

OUR REVIEW OF THE BROWN family's situation in Chapter 16 gave you an introduction to the type of data that goes into the Family Financial Projection (our spreadsheets) and the information you'll get out of it. In this chapter, we'll take a closer look at this analysis tool; in Chapter 18 we'll use it to evaluate a few more family examples.

If you really don't like computers and financial analysis, you may want to move right on to Chapter 18, but we urge you to at least scan this chapter first. We talk less about computers and programs than about how the analysis is structured and what is included.

The process of creating a long-term net-worth plan may look forbidding. It certainly is not a back-of-the-envelope operation. But with today's software and personal computers, it is doable. And the rewards of having a plan in place are well worth the time spent. It will not only allow you to become comfortable with a certain level of charitable giving, but will also help ease your concerns about running out of money during your lifetime.

It can be relatively easy to calculate individual pieces of a financial analysis, but it is quite difficult to develop a comprehensive financial plan in which all the significant factors are brought together into one overview. Likewise, it is hard to reach key gifting decisions if you don't have a good picture of your whole financial situation.

As we began to do major gifting ourselves, we worked out a spreadsheet program that gave us a good overview of our projected financial situation and the level of giving we would be comfortable with. When we started writing this book, we expanded and refined our spreadsheet to make it more comprehensive and more general. The program that we will discuss in this chapter is the result of our evolutionary process. We think it important to note that we developed this approach in direct response to a donor family's need for information. That is why we think it will probably address your need for information as well.

We certainly didn't want to endure the kind of personal punishment involved in writing a major program, nor did we crave the ego satisfaction that such program design might deliver. Instead, we tried to adapt one of the commercially available packages to our needs. We were not successful in doing that. In the end, working with Bill Rogers, we did it ourselves.

We were guided in our efforts by these six requirements:

- **The analysis must be comprehensive.** The core elements of long-term financial planning interact with each other. For the results of any analysis to be of much value, all of the significant financial issues—such as net worth, income, spending, and tax calculations—needed to be included and set within a long-term time frame.

- **The approach has to be structured.** Any long-term look at a comprehensive financial plan must, by definition, contain a lot of data and calculations. For the information to be usable, it needs to be organized in a linear fashion, as intuitive as possible, so that readers (and their accountants) can work their way through it.

- **Assumptions must be clear.** The input assumptions have a fundamental impact on the results of any analysis. Therefore, we knew that it had to be easy to see what the assumptions were, to alter these assumptions for comparative purposes, and to reflect changes in an individual's situation.

* **Calculations must be traceable.** For the program to have credibility, the more sophisticated users would need to be able to work their way through the "code" and see how the calculations were made.

* **Conclusions must be clear.** Although there are a lot of input assumptions and some fairly complex calculations in the program, the results and conclusions needed to be presented in a straightforward way that would allow users to see clearly what the program was telling them.

* **The effort must be focused.** There are a lot of factors floating about the world of financial analysis. To make this analysis tool serve our purposes, we had to keep it focused on the primary goals, otherwise it would have become quite unwieldy and ultimately unusable.

Why This Program?

Given how many commercial (and relatively user-friendly) financial management programs there are on the market, why did we develop our own? More important, why should you consider using it? As noted above, we looked and could not find an existing program that did what we needed. So we did it ourselves. If you happen to come across a commercial program that does this job well, please let us know. We would be happy to retire from the software business! In the meantime, these are the advantages our program offers:

It is focused and inclusive. It concentrates on the needs of well-to-do people who want a long-term financial overview as a basis for determining timing, methods, amounts, and tax implications of lifetime distribution of significant portions of their net worth. Nothing more, nothing less.

It is accessible. The program is a Microsoft Excel spreadsheet set up to run on a Windows PC. It is available for download on the Internet. (Please see Appendix A for specifics.) If you are fairly computer-literate and have access to a reasonably up-to-date personal computer, you'll be able to load the program, plug in your own data, and see how it works for your situation. If you aren't comfortable doing this type of analysis or don't have time for it, there are accountants out there who would be happy to do it for you.

It is adaptable. You are free to use this program in any number of ways. For instance:

- **Observe the results.** You can look at the summary of inputs and outputs that has been printed as part of this book, reach some conclusions as to where you fall in the range of examples we offer, and use one of them as a place to start for creating your own analyses.

- **Observe the organization.** You can look at how the problem was approached, the asset categories that we used, and the type of detail that we included. That may trigger some thoughts on how you would like to view your own long-term assets-distribution plan.

- **Extract elements of data and calculation.** You will find that the tax calculations can be extracted as a reference for less-global calculations. The tax table included in the program is also quite usable for the layman.

- ❧ **The spreadsheets can be used as a basis for discussion with your financial advisors.** You can look at the results, decide whether this input/output method of looking at your affairs works for you, and then take the results to your financial advisors. You can tell them that you'd like to see your financial life laid out in a similar fashion and see what they can come up with.

- ❧ **Play with it.** Those who are computer savvy can load the program and then work with it. After all, it was created by a computer-savvy (and somewhat compulsive) non-programmer, so although it is a big program, it is not terribly sophisticated. (If Dick can do it, you can do it!) It does follow an intuitive logic.

- ❧ **Use it as a jumping-off point.** As you get into it, you may find that the program is okay, but you would like to improve it to more fully meet your needs. Please do.

We think that this program is good but certainly not the only way to accomplish the necessary analysis task. Most financial advisors have some type of financial-planning software that works for them and, we presume, for their clients. Be it home-grown, supplied by their corporate headquarters, or an adaptation of commercially available software, your advisors no doubt have a computer analysis tool that they are comfortable with. By all means use their program, *so long as it gives you what you need to know as a potential major donor.* The key tests, we think, of the appropriateness of the program you use are "Is it comprehensive, is it focused, are the input assumptions stated clearly, and are the conclusions presented in a manner that helps your major gifting strategic planning?"

18
Baseline Data for Six Families

IN THIS CHAPTER we're going to explore the situations of six very different families. Before we introduce you to our sample families, we'd like to tell you a little about how we selected the data that went into each family's financial profile. We wanted to create earning, growth, and spending patterns that seemed appropriate for the level of wealth of each family. We assigned gifting levels that seemed realistic, given each family's situation, maintaining the necessary net-worth reserve ("enough") while working to give as much as seemed prudent. Just like real life.

The Six Families

We will be comparing the analysis of the finances for six hypothetical couples:

1. The Allens, who are "comfortable";
2. The Browns (yes, we repeat their data here), who are "very comfortable";
3. The Clarks, who are "rich";
4. The Drakes, who are "solid citizens";
5. The Emorys who are also "rich"; and
6. The Finches, who have "great potential."

These made-up families will help us personalize our exploration of a number of levels of wealth and understand how gifting or not gifting affects their long-term financial situations. The purpose of this approach is to give the reader a

Table 18-1: Starting Data for Six Families

	1. ALLEN	2. BROWN	3. CLARK	4. DRAKE	5. EMORY	6. FINCH
Starting year	2000	2000	2000	2000	2000	2000
Age at start	60	60	60	60	70	45
Age at death	90	90	90	90	100	75
Total return expectation	9%	9%	9%	6%	6%	12%
Net worth						
Investments	400,000	800,000	2,000,000	300,000	2,000,000	50,000
Retirement accounts	400,000	700,000	1,500,000	300,000	1,500,000	50,000
Real estate equity	200,000	300,000	300,000	200,000	300,000	50,000
Life insurance	500,000	700,000	1,200,000	400,000	1,200,000	100,000
Total net worth	1,500,000	2,500,000	5,000,000	1,200,000	5,000,000	250,000
Annual gifting						
Family	10,000	20,000	60,000	2,000	25,000	1,000
Charity	10,000	28,000	70,000	2,000	23,000	2,000
Total annual gifting	20,000	48,000	130,000	4,000	48,000	3,000
Annual living expenses	75,000	90,000	150,000	50,000	110,000	55,000
Expected inheritance or other deposit	250,000	500,000	1,000,000	100,000	500,000	5,000,000
"Enough"	1,000,000	2,000,000	2,500,000	850,000	2,500,000	3,000,000

Reference: Appendix Table A-2, Tables B-1 through Tables B-6

quick look at a range of situations, one of which they might directly relate to. Our hope is that the reader will then be intrigued enough to take the next step and consider how these approaches might fit their own situation.

The Families

The key similarity between the six families is that their basic needs are well covered and that their net worth (without gifting) is projected to grow in the future. They have money to spare or can at least project that they will. Each family is a couple. This is not a slight to single folks, but rather a compromise we made for programming simplicity. For the same reason, we have decreed that both partners were born on January 1 of the same year and that both will die on January 1 some 30 years later.

We have laid out the basic financial assumptions for all six families in TABLE 18-1. You will find much more detail on these assumptions in Appendix B, but what's been included here is the core data. (If you've just joined our discussion of financial analysis, you may want to refer back to Chapter 16, where we introduced and explained this format.)

Table 18-1: Starting Data for Six Families

Our first three families (the Allens, Browns, and Clarks) have net worths ranging from $1,500,000 to $5,000,000, including life insurance. The common denominator here is that these three families are relatively aggressive equity investors, expecting an average total return (income plus growth) on their investments of 9% per year.

Investing philosophy. We couldn't resist throwing in a few words here on investing philosophy. The conventional wisdom is that as we get older, our investment portfolio should become more and more conservative (more bonds, fewer stocks), so that the potential for volatility is diminished and the risk of loss is reduced. That may well be appropriate for many, but if your assets are well above what you need ("enough") and if your nature will allow you to tolerate significant year-to-year volatility, we suggest that you consider keeping a significant long-term equity investment position.

By any longer-term historical measure, stocks (ownership in a company) have done better for investors than bonds (loans to a company or to a government entity) insofar as total return is concerned. The price you pay for staying with stocks is the possibility of increased volatility on a year-to-year basis. The long-term reward is that you may be able to give much more to your family and your chosen charities because of higher total returns on those investments.

This is certainly not meant as investment advice; we are only suggesting that you and your financial advisors should consider this option if it fits your situation. We think it's important to remember that the conventional wisdom we read about so often in the popular press is aimed at the average couple, and if you fall into the wealth categories discussed in this book you may be quite far from "average." We suggest that you keep an open mind on this point.

The Drakes and the Emorys are cautious investors. They have the bulk of their money in income-producing investments (bonds perhaps) and are projecting a much lower total return on their investments. Therefore, their estates are projected to grow quite modestly. The Drakes need to be very cautious about their level of annual gifting, but certainly a significant level of bequest at their death is worthy of consideration.

The Emorys are very well-to-do and could give somewhat more. However, their giving is constrained by the fact that their asset base is not growing very much.

The Finches are quite a different matter. They are only 45 years old, but they expect to become "wealthy" in the near future. Mr. Finch is a founding partner in a software startup company that is showing great promise. He expects to cash out for a bundle in the year 2007. The Finches are comfortable with risk and expect their investments (long term) to generate an annual total return well above average.

As you look at the tables, you can see that we assigned reasonable levels for salary and wages. All of our families are still working at least part time at their "starting age," except for the Emorys, who have fully retired from income-producing employment at age 70. They are the only couple old enough to be getting social security at the starting year of the analysis.

It is important to note that although we are using net worth as a shorthand for defining wealth, it is only part of the story. We would need to know total return (growth and income) on investments, the portion of income from other sources, and the degree of spending that a family does in order to more effectively define wealth. (We talk quite a bit about this issue in Chapter 20.) But for our purposes in this chapter, we will simply use net worth to categorize levels of wealth.

As we have noted, "enough" is the amount that each couple has determined that they need to retain in their net-worth column in order to be comfortable as they get older. This also has a growth factor built into it. Each couple does some annual gifting. We have selected gifting levels that fit with the level of extra estate value that is being generated each year.

19
Financial Summaries for Six Families

IN THIS CHAPTER, we will examine the results of a lifetime of "giving" for each of the six families. These results are tied to the basic premise noted at the start of the book—that what you don't spend, you will give to family, to charity, and to the government (taxes).

To get in the right frame of mind for reviewing these analyses, picture yourself lying on your deathbed, reviewing what you accomplished with your money during your lifetime. (We warned you that you needed to be comfortable with your own mortality to use this book!) Being a methodical person, you'll have some summary spreadsheets at hand showing the accumulated totals that you gave to family and friends, charity, and taxes over last 30 years of your life and at your death.

As you review those final spreadsheets, you might think to yourself, "I wish I had had a chance to look at these numbers 30 years ago; I'll bet I would have made some changes"—but unfortunately it's too late now. Ah, but then you wake up! It was only a dream. It is not 30 years from now, it is today and you can make those changes. Read on.

What Did Our Six Families Do with Their Money?

We have set up these families to show how some basic economic assumptions would play out over a 30-year period in different family situations. You may find a situation here that is similar to yours. If your situation is not closely represented here, jump right in and enter your own baseline data in the downloaded spreadsheet program and see how your specific lifetime totals work out.

Summary Results in Table Form

TABLES 19-1 and 19-2 show summary results of the six family's financial actions, "with" and "without" gifting options, over a 30-year projected life expectancy.

As you look at the data results, you'll see some interesting patterns. In each case the couple can make a choice to do or not do major gifting during their lifetimes. *With* gifting they are able to give quite a lot to charity; *without* gifting, they "give" to taxes. In each case, their net worth stays above the "enough" level, whether they give or not.

If our more aggressive investors—the Allens, Browns, Clarks, and Finches—do not give, their net worth goes way up. In fact, without gifting, the Finches' net worth goes into the stratosphere. If our conservative investors—the Drakes and Emorys—do not give, their net worth grows, but not all that much.

Let's take a closer look at the Finches, our really big-bucks couple. Although some of their financial patterns are similar to those of the other five families, the Finches are truly a special case. Because their estate is projected to grow so large, and because they are relatively young at the time they become wealthy, the long-term impact of their choices is different. Note that *without* gifting, their estate becomes very large at age 75, with a real probability of another 15 to 20 years of estate growth before they die. This is serious lawyer and financial advisor country. We would urge the Finches to become deeply involved with the professional estate planning and philanthropy community

Table 19-1: Lifetime Summaries for the Allen, Brown, and Clark Families

	1 ALLEN		2 BROWN		3 CLARK	
	with gifting	*without gifting*	*with gifting*	*without gifting*	*with gifting*	*without gifting*
Net worth						
Starting	1,500,000	1,500,000	2,500,000	2,500,000	5,000,000	5,000,000
Ending	2,300,000	4,300,000	4,800,000	10,400,000	9,700,000	24,200,000
"Enough"						
Starting	1,000,000	1,000,000	2,000,000	2,000,000	2,500,000	2,500,000
Ending	1,800,000	1,800,000	3,600,000	3,600,000	4,400,000	4,400,000
Lifetime gifting						
Taxes	1,400,000	3,200,000	2,700,000	8,700,000	6,000,000	21,200,000
Charity	700,000	0	3,400,000	0	9,500,000	0
Family	2,300,000	2,800,000	3,500,000	5,400,000	6,400,000	11,300,000
Total lifetime giving	4,400,000	6,000,000	9,600,000	14,100,000	21,900,000	32,500,000
Lifetime taxes						
Income	1,000,000	1,400,000	1,800,000	2,900,000	3,900,000	6,400,000
Capital Gains	250,000	370,000	350,000	800,000	770,000	1,960,000
Estate	100,000	1,500,000	600,000	5,000,000	1,400,000	12,800,000
Total lifetime taxes	1,350,000	3,270,000	2,750,000	8,700,000	6,070,000	21,160,000

Reference: Appendix Figure C-1 through C-6, Table D-1 through Table D-6, Table E-1 through E-6

Table 19-1: Lifetime Summaries for the Drake, Emory, and Finch Families

	4 DRAKE		5 EMORY		6 FINCH	
	with gifting	*without gifting*	*with gifting*	*without gifting*	*with gifting*	*without gifting*
Net worth						
Starting	1,200,000	1,200,000	5,000,000	5,000,000	300,000	300,000
Ending	1,800,000	2,100,000	4,000,000	7,200,000	8,400,000	42,200,000
"Enough"						
Starting	900,000	900,000	2,500,000	2,500,000	3,000,000	3,000,000
Ending	1,500,000	1,500,000	4,400,000	4,400,000	5,300,000	5,300,000
Lifetime gifting						
Taxes	1,000,000	1,400,000	4,500,000	8,200,000	6,100,000	28,900,000
Charity	800,000	0	2,100,000	0	13,000,000	0
Family	1,300,000	1,900,000	3,800,000	4,300,000	9,400,000	19,900,000
Total lifetime giving	3,100,000	3,300,000	10,400,000	12,500,000	28,500,000	48,800,000
Lifetime taxes						
Income	900,000	1,000,000	3,300,000	4,400,000	600,000	3,600,000
Capital Gains	120,000	130,000	630,000	860,000	2,160,000	3,030,000
Estate	0	300,000	600,000	2,900,000	3,400,000	22,300,000
Total lifetime taxes	1,020,000	1,430,000	4,530,000	8,160,000	6,160,000	28,930,000

Reference: Appendix Figure C-1 through C-6, Table D-1 through Table D-6, Table E-1 through E-6 and to do it fairly soon. Now is a good time for them to start the learning process. They are certainly headed for the financial territory where using the most sophisticated tax planning tools would probably be wise to consider.

Looking at the data for our sample families, we can see that in most cases, if the family does major gifting during their lifetimes, their accumulative tax bill is greatly reduced, and their gifting to charity becomes significant. In oversimplified terms, the reasons for this dramatic difference are fairly straightforward.

- As an estate gets above the $2,000,000 to $3,000,000 range, the 55% estate tax rate comes into play and the estate tax grows rapidly. (For estates over $10,000,000 the effective estate tax rate takes another jump. This "over $10,000" factor is not reflected in the program.)

- As the estate gets larger, it is likely that funds remaining in a retirement account will be taxed at a very high rate (70% to 90% perhaps).

- If one gives at a regular rate on a year-to-year basis, normal tax deductions that one can receive are quite effective in reducing income taxes, capital gains taxes, and estate taxes.

This supports the key point made earlier, that you can have a great deal of control over where your "gifting" goes, depending on when you give and how you choose to do it.

Take a few minutes (well, maybe a *lot* of minutes) to study the patterns shown here. You can refer back to the discussion in Chapter 16 to refresh your memory on the categories. What surprised us was how effective regular annual giving was at reducing taxes. That was true even for our more modestly wealthy families. This shows that these techniques are not just options for the "really rich." These steady and simple gifting techniques hold significant tax benefits for a growing part of the population.

The Finches are, again, a very different case. They give only $3,000 because they can only spare $3,000 in the year 2000. But they will make it up many times over in the years ahead. Hats off to them for thinking about it now and planning for it.

And the Message Is . . .

Our six-family analysis leads to a number of general observations. Fundamentally, the message seems to be this: The family that has (or expects to have) wealth in excess of what they need to cover living, healthcare, and long-life contingencies *and* that has an income, asset growth, and spending pattern that will allow their net worth to grow over and above this "enough" level into the future can choose to:

1. Give steadily to family and charity from the assets over and above the "enough" level during their lifetimes rather than allowing roughly the same amount go to taxes.

2. Not give during their lifetimes and instead see those assets go to the government as income tax, capital gains tax, and estate tax.

Section Four

THE
SUMMARY

20
It All Comes Together

CONGRATULATIONS—you have worked your way through a lot of material. Our challenge, and we suspect yours as well, has been how to organize all of these pieces into some kind of a comprehensive mental picture that will help you design your own major-gifting program.

Our conclusions on the gifting tools and techniques have been fairly well laid out in Section 2, so we'll not dwell more on that part. Also, Section 3 pretty much says all we have to say on the analysis side of things. However, we will add a few words on the issue of "Who is qualified to become a major donor?" But mostly our summary deals with the personal side of major gifting and the highlights of what this process has taught us.

Who Is Qualified to Be a Major Donor?

Most of us probably think that someone has to be wealthy in order to become a major donor to charity, family, and friends. If you were to ask another person what the term "wealthy" means, you would likely get a ready answer. However, if you ask ten people to define "wealthy," you are likely to get ten different answers.

To some, anyone who lives in a big house is wealthy. To others, anyone with a net worth of a million dollars or more is wealthy, or anyone who makes $100,000 per year is wealthy. The truth is, none of these usual definitions of wealth are very helpful in identifying potential major donors.

We suggest that the term "wealthy" be retired as a qualifying definition for someone who is able to take part in major gifting. Instead, substitute the term "qualified." (Not flashy, but it gets to the heart of the issue.)

We think that you are qualified to be a major donor if you meet the following criteria.

1. You have sound sources of cash available for required spending, both now and in the future. This might be regular income, cash from sale of assets, or some combination of the two.

2. You have assets or cash in reserve (savings, investments, house equity, insurance, and so on) to cover any serious financial needs that might crop up.

3. Your net worth is *growing* year by year, over and above the rate of inflation.

In other words, the qualifier is not how much we own or how much we earn, but the combination of both in relation to how much we spend and how much we feel we need to keep in reserve. There are no specific numbers attached to this definition of "qualified."

The implication is, of course, that you don't need to be rich to become a major donor during your lifetime. Conversely, you may be viewed as "rich" according to exterior indications (high salary, high-consumption lifestyle) and yet you may not be "qualified" to give away any money at all. (We recommend that you read *The Millionaire Next Door* which explores this whole subject, if you haven't already.)

Viewed another way, potential major donors might have a great pension, good health insurance and life insurance, and lead a fairly conservative lifestyle. They might also have a relatively modest net worth, perhaps a home that's paid for, and some savings. These folks probably wouldn't consider themselves to be "rich," but because their needs are so well-covered by ongoing income, their reserve needs are well-covered by insurance, and their spending is at a relatively modest level, they might be very well qualified to become major donors.

A second couple, on the other hand, may have a high income, live a very visible and prosperous lifestyle, but have very little bottom-line net worth. While appearing "rich" to the outside world, they would likely not be good candidates for becoming major donors.

Yet another couple might have virtually no "income" at all, but could own a closet-full of excellent growth stocks. Their high net worth (some of which could easily be "harvested" to produce cash for living on a year-to-year basis) might easily qualify them to become major donors.

Are you a candidate for becoming a major donor?

A Look into the Future

We have come to view the gifting process as a lifetime activity. We have learned that many of the simple and powerful tax-advantaged gifting techniques work best when used in conjunction with a regular, annual, long-term gifting program. We have certainly found that we get a great sense of reward from having an ongoing role in the donor process.

Therefore, we have our financial affairs set up so that we can monitor our situation on a year-to-year basis and make annual adjustments to our gifting plan. We expect that at our deaths, the estate taxes will be moderate because we plan to give steadily from our estate to family, friends, and nonprofit organizations, keeping our estate at a level where estate taxes will not be a significant factor.

We realize that many people, as they age, become more set in their ways, more fearful, more inward-looking, less interested in new experiences, and less comfortable with complication in their lives. Any or all of these factors can tend to make a person less giving. Will this happen to us? Perhaps.

To us, this probability points out just one more advantage in having done our research and having created this long-term gifting program. It will help to ensure that our current inclination to give will be sustained as we get older.

We wouldn't want to give up the sense of reward that we get from being participants in the gifting process, even though our degree of hands-on involvement may change. We think the framework we have put in place will be sustainable and will stand the test of time.

Views on Privacy

Shortly after our inheritance came to us, we sat in Bill Rogers' office and, almost in a whisper, said, "Is there some way we can give money and not have anyone know about it?" We were very concerned about people knowing we had money, both because we are private people and because we didn't want to get on "everyone's list."

Little by little, that view changed. It did not change overnight, that's for sure. Now a lot of people know we give away money, and things haven't changed much. We don't get more mail asking for donations than we did in the past. We think the neighbors know perfectly well that we have some spare money, and they still tolerate us quite well. And here we are, three years later, writing a book about giving away money and sharing thoughts that we never thought we would share. We would never have guessed it.

The List

We think the following list captures the basics of what we have learned and the insights we have gained as we have worked through the process.

The Basics

- ❧ You will give away what you don't spend; the only questions are how, when, and to whom.
- ❧ Taxes are a factor, but not the only factor.
- ❧ In all things, relationships reign supreme.
- ❧ Objectives first, tools and techniques later.
- ❧ We all want some form of control over our gifting; the nature and degree of control will vary for each individual.
- ❧ Being smart in how you give will enhance the effect of your caring.
- ❧ Give during your lifetime—enjoy the process!

Advisors and Advice

- ❧ Search for advisors who embrace your values; they are out there.
- ❧ Question the conventional wisdom; it may not be right for you.
- ❧ Work with your advisors; you'll be glad you did.

Family

- ❧ Seek to do no harm.
- ❧ A well-written estate plan is a great gift to your family.
- ❧ Putting your family members "in business" with each

other may not be a good idea, no matter what the tax savings might be.

❦ For some situations, a family trust is a very good idea.

Nonprofits

❦ Well-run nonprofits are very effective at managing the resources that are given to them.

❦ Looking for great people? Visit the nonprofits.

Tools and Techniques

❦ Give to the government or give to charity—the choice is largely yours.

❦ Start with the simple options, work up to the complex choices.

❦ Just because you can, doesn't mean you should.

❦ Large tax savings can be realized using simple gifting tools and techniques

❦ Think about bequesting your tax deferred retirement plan to charity. Big tax savings potential here.

Business and Financial Issues

❦ Knowledge is freedom; know thy numbers.

❦ Keep an open mind about selling or gifting capital.

Taxes

❦ The government rewards charitable gifting, up to a point.

❦ The government penalizes family gifting, beyond a point.

* Keeping the size of your estate in check is a key way to avoid estate taxes.

* Capital Gains taxes and Income taxes can be greatly reduced by appropriate gifting.

Money and Strategies

* You may be "richer" than you think. If your assets are growing steadily, do a life projection of your probable total assets at your date of death. You may be quite surprised.

* Review your investment strategy. It may be more conservative than you need, and your charities and family will be the losers for it.

* By giving on a yearly basis, you can pay far less in taxes, give substantial amounts to charity, and still leave a lot to your family.

* If you don't want to give to charity during your lifetime, but you would still like to have your estate save a lot on taxes, hang on to your money and bequest it at your death.

Recognition and Rewards

* Recognition is an external thing. Reward is internal.

* Some people want general public recognition, others do not.

* Everyone looks for a sense of reward from their gifting. The type of "reward" may differ.

* Being known as a donor may not be so bad.

A Life-Enhancing Experience

We have been gifting for a number of years now. We have learned a lot, and our views have changed a great deal. Much to our surprise, the task of gifting money (and time) has taken a much more central place in our lives then we would have predicted. Our involvement in giving has supported and enhanced a positive outlook and sense of a full life.

We have found that giving money away isn't a painful process at all. In fact, it is quite rewarding. It is great to know that someone might be in a little less pain (physical or mental) as a result of our efforts. The people we have met as part of our philanthropic involvement have enhanced our lives. It comforts us to know that the personal values of the family members we have lost live on through our efforts. We feel grateful that our family members will be able to have a fuller life because of the money we have shared with them.

We have found that becoming major donors has had some subtle (and positive) impacts on our spending habits that we did not anticipate. Maintaining a reasonable degree of gifting makes us more comfortable with our net worth and more comfortable spending on ourselves because we know we are also contributing to the needs of others.

A question to ponder. How many wealthy people are unhappy people? Quite a few, we understand. Would sharing their good fortune enhance their total sense of well being? We think so, and we think a number of objective studies have shown this to be true.

We don't feel that the desire to give time and money to useful causes is limited to a group with a special calling. Some people have money to give and others have time to give. Some have both. And there are great needs out there for both volunteers and funding. The rewards of giving are very real, and we believe that they are out there for everyone.

We have found no disadvantages to charitable giving, save perhaps the fact that our lives are so full that some home projects remain in need of attention. We guess this is a "disadvantage" to be coveted, when we think about it. So far we have seen no disadvantages to the gifting process. None.

In Conclusion

Welcome to the world of major gifting. It has enhanced our lives far more than we would ever have guessed. We wish for you a similar experience.

Appendixes

Appendix A
The Family Financial
Program: An Overview

As we have noted in various places in the book, we feel that the core to a sustainable major-gifting program is a sound projection of your long-term financial situation. The Family Financial Program provides just that. This spreadsheet program is available to you on the Internet at:

www.smartandcaring.com

All the worksheets, tables, and graphs shown or referred to in this book are included with the program. The download also supplies some operating instructions. Do take a look at it, as you just may find some updated material.

This first appendix section looks at the mechanics of the program in some detail. This discussion assumes that the reader is familiar with the basic concepts of spreadsheets, but it does not require a great depth of knowledge of the inner workings of a spreadsheet to understand what is being discussed.

As you move into the area where we suggest that you boot up the spreadsheet and work through its specifics, you will probably find that a more advanced level of spreadsheet knowledge will serve you well. Although the spreadsheet is big, each element of it is fairly straightforward, and we have worked to make its flow as intuitive as possible. In any case, be prepared for a significant time commitment once you enter the spreadsheet—it covers a lot of territory.

We will not be giving you an in-depth explanation of the cell-by-cell coding details that underlie the spreadsheet. However, we do plan on giving you an overview of its structure and intent. Basically, we will leave you to take up the challenge of exploring such program details on your own. As you might expect, we won't be able to offer technical support of any kind.

In its pristine condition, the spreadsheet contains all the data necessary to produce all the examples shown in the book. You can substitute your own numbers as you see fit. One of the major advantages of a computerized spreadsheet is that it invites running "what if" trials; this spreadsheet is no exception. In fact, the program is structured to invite that kind of experimentation.

We have included hard-copy samples of input and output worksheets discussed in this appendix. If you want hard-copy printout of other scenarios or of the "main" worksheet, you can boot up the program and print them out. This may not be as user-friendly as we've come to expect from shrink-wrapped software, but manipulating the spreadsheets is really doable if you work at it.

The program consists of a number of worksheets. You will find samples of most of them in this appendix. As we discuss each one, you'll be able to follow along using those sample printouts, which can be found in the appendix references.

Table A-1: Starting Page ("START")

This page accepts selection of family and gifting options. It shows macros available for running the program and printing the worksheets.

Error messages. The program does not have a sophisticated error-checking capability. If you put in numbers that are not logical (such as spending more money than you have or expecting a 25% average return on your investments over 30 years), it is likely to produce some odd-looking summary results. If you get strange results, go back and check the logic of your data inputs—the problem is likely to be there. We have built in a few error-checking messages that will give you a hint that there is a problem with inputs and you should go look for the cause of trouble, but they are the exceptions, not the rule. The worst problem with errors, of course, would be if you put in illogical data, but the program accepted it for some reason, and the output still looked okay. You might then accept the output data as fact and perhaps even act on that information. That could put you in real trouble.

Our point, of course, is that you must bear the full responsibility for acting on the results of your spreadsheet calculations. We would never recommend that anyone attempt to use this program for more than it is intended for; it is only meant to serve as a strategy-planning tool. We strongly urge you not to take any specific financial actions without the independent review of your own qualified professional advisors.

Table A-2: Starting Data ("DATA1")

This worksheet is a good one to use for stepping back and studying the big picture, seeing how the family options compare with each other. (It prints from the macro noted on "START.") It includes half the data input for the six families that is required to run the full program. (The other half shows up in TABLE A-3: Lifetime Data.)

You'll find that you can easily replace the data for the families in columns 1, 2, 3, 4, 5, and 6 with your personal data, without having to get deeply into the details of the spreadsheet. We encourage you to start by trying this approach first. You may be surprised at how much information the spreadsheet can give you without your having to get into heavy program detail.

You'll see that the first column at the top of the worksheet is labeled "Current Run." Don't enter data in this column! When the program runs, it will read the family selection you made on TABLE A-1: Starting Page (1, 2, 3, 4, 5, or 6) and automatically copy that family's data into the "Current Run" column. You may, however, change any of the data in the dashed boxes under "Enter Family Data Here." In fact, feel free to modify the numbers in these boxes to your heart's content, and print out the new results.

The data-entry categories are listed along the left axis. This is the same data that you saw, in summary form, in Chapter 16, where we described the Brown family's situation, and in Chapter 18, where we examined all six of the family examples. Here we include the full input data. We'll explain the categories one by one:

Family

Number. This is a reference number that will help you keep track of which family option you are dealing with.

Name. The name is mainly meant to help personalize the family categories.

Description. This field provides room for a few words characterizing each example.

Age and Time Factors

Current year. The year you want the analysis to begin.

Starting age. The family's age at the beginning of the analysis period.

Age at death. The family's age, 30 years later.

Net Worth Accounts

(A) Investments—Other. This includes all your conventional investments, other than retirement plans. It does not include real estate or insurance.

Growth percentage. This is the average annual growth you expect these investments to realize over the next 30 years. This is where the "what if" capability of the program comes in to play. You may want plug in some alternate growth numbers to see how such changes effect the overall results.

Income percentage. This field is similar in function; you can plug in different estimates of how much income you expect to realize from your investments.

Background on Retirement Accounts. The investment and tax aspects of retirement accounts are very different from those of conventional investments. There are huge tax implications here, so you need to look at these accounts separately in order to understand the impact they will have on your long-term financial situation. But first, let's touch on some background information.

As you know, a qualified retirement plan enjoys special treatment under the tax laws. As the years go by, a retirement plan is permitted to grow without your having to take any distributions of income or growth, and without your having to pay any taxes on either income or capital gains. The beauty of it is that the government lets you keep the money for the long term, while it grows and grows. But the day of reckoning awaits. When you take some or all of it out, you will have to pay income taxes on all of it, including deposits and accumulated growth and income.

There are four typical conditions under which you or your estate may receive funds from your qualified retirement plans. First, you may take some or all of the funds out before you reach age 59 ^{1}/$_2$. This is generally not a considered a wise thing to do, since you will pay a high penalty (10% at this writing). Second, you may make withdrawals after age 59 ^{1}/$_2$ without a penalty. You will, however, owe income taxes on those funds at your then-current rate.

Third, you *must* begin to make withdrawals when you reach age 70 ^{1}/$_2$. The rate of these minimum withdrawals will rise over time, as specified by the IRS, based on some rather complex calculations. We have included a typical withdrawal rate table (see TABLE A-4: Tax Tables) to serve as a general example of the principles at work. If you get really serious about this, ask your CPA to calculate the table for your specific situation. As a rule, the percentage of withdrawal starts out low at age 70$^{1}/_{2}$ and builds to the point that you will have had to withdraw it all by roughly age 90 (and will have paid a lot of income tax on those funds in the process).

Fourth, you can die with the account (or some of it) still not withdrawn. At this point your estate will face two combined tax hits. There will be income taxes on the full amount, plus estate taxes, also on the full amount, if the combined total of your estate is up in the estate-tax range. The combined hit can be as much as 40 to 90% of the total retirement plan, as we are determined to point out incessantly!

The tax implications of these accounts and the variability on when these funds may be withdrawn have led us to the approach we've taken for our calculations regarding retirement plans. First, we have split them into two categories.

- **(B1) Retirement Accounts (Distributed).** This is the amount you have taken out of the retirement account(s). We treat this distributed amount as if it were retained as a separate account, for clarity of calculation, even though in practice most of us would probably co-mingle these withdrawn funds with our regular investments.

- **(B2) Retirement Accounts (Undistributed).** This is the account value for the amount remaining in your active, qualified retirement plan(s). Important Note! The programming assumes that you are planning to bequeath all of your retirement plan assets, both the part that remains active within the plan and the part that has already been distributed from the plan. In other words, the assets in both (B1) and (B2) will go to charity at your death, if you have selected the "with gifting" option.

We have separated these accounts because a thoughtful investor should certainly be treating them differently. Good tax-management would lead wise investors (that's you, of course) to satisfy their needs for funds (to spend or give) by using the following withdrawal priority: First, you would likely withdraw assets from your *(A) Regular Investments* category, down to a point, leaving you retirement assets in your tax-deferred plan. (Most of us have a minimum level of regular investments that we wish to maintain. We take that minimum into consideration in the program.)

After reaching the minimum level of (A) investments, we wise investors would next be likely to withdraw assets that have been distributed from our qualified retirement plan. (After these assets have been withdrawn and income taxes have been paid, the funds no longer enjoy any special tax treatment. From the IRS's point of view, withdrawn retirement plan assets may as well be co-mingled with your other assets—they don't care.)

Third, we wise investors are likely to then look at withdrawing assets from our qualified retirement plans, assuming that we are over age 59 1/2 and don't face the heavy penalties that earlier withdrawal would engender.

The spreadsheet program reflects this priority of assets withdrawal. It is programmed to first take assets from the *(A) Investments—Other* accounts (down to the "minimum retained" level), then from the *(B1) Retirement Accounts (Distributed)* until they are exhausted, and finally from the *(B2) Retirement Accounts (Undistributed)*. We have programmed in assumed growth and income assumptions for the (B1) and (B2) accounts.

(C) Real Estate Equity. We show current real estate equity and a projected growth percentage of this equity.

(D) Life Insurance Amount. Note that there are major tax implications depending on whether your life insurance policies have been set up to be owned by your estate or have been excluded from your estate. Also, as we have noted in Chapter 16, we use "face value" rather than "cash value" in the analysis. See your professional advisors to find out where you stand on life insurance.

Total Net Worth. This row provides totals for all the net-worth columns.

"Enough." This is the minimum base net worth that the donor would like to retain. It is calculated to grow a specified annual rate, typically equal to inflation. It is good to remember that as you get much older, the "enough" level may not need to keep growing at the same rate. That's because your spending many contract or at least not continue to grow steadily year after year. (For example, we will probably be taking fewer skiing vacations as we get into our late 80s.)

Minimum to be Retained in (A) Investments. As noted above, we have assumed that the typical donor would like to retain a minimum amount in the basic (A) investment category. This is where that minimum is recorded.

Tax Rates. These are the assumed blended tax rates used in the spreadsheet calculations.

Other. This category includes three estimates:

- *Annual Inflation.* No one knows for sure, of course, but we give it our best guess.

- *Capital Sold (Subject to Capital Gains Tax).* This is an assumption of what portion of the annual growth from your regular (A) investments would be sold off each year and would therefore be subject to capital gains taxes. For the very active (and successful) equity investors who do a lot of trading, the percentage could be much higher than the estimate provided as a default. For very stable investors who buy and hold, with little trading, it might be much lower.

* *Capital Gains Realized on Typical Capital Sale.*

Table A-3: Lifetime Data ("DATA2")

This worksheet contains the second half of the input data for a given run. You don't enter data on this sheet, the computer will enter it for you from one of the six data-entry sheets. To change this data; you first go to one of the "Six Families' Lifetime Data" sheets, and enter the specific input data there. (You can get to these by clicking the spreadsheet tabs at the bottom of your Excel screen. They are OPT1 for Family 1, OPT2 for Family 2, and so on.)

Then, when the program is run, the computer takes the data from the specified data input sheet ("OPT2" for the Brown Family, for instance) and copies it over to TABLE A-3: Lifetime Data ("DATA2"). The computer uses this information as the input for this particular run.

The reason for this is approach is that it lets you keep as many as six family scenarios in memory, allowing you to move back and forth among them, modifying and comparing, without having to go back and reenter a lot of data for each "what if" trial.

The first two columns at the left of TABLE A-3 show the year of the analysis and the age of the couple during that year. Across the top of this worksheet, you will see four categories of data.

Other Income. This category is broken down into *Salary and Wages, Misc. Income, Pension, and Total Other Income.* Using the Brown family example, the numbers show that the Browns are in semi-retirement at age 60, working part-time to bring in Salary and Wages in the year 2000. For the next five years, the Browns work a little less each year, and their Salary and Wages will steadily drop through the year 2006.

At age 65 they both decide that enough is enough, and they are no longer going to work for wages. (They are spending more time working free for nonprofits, no doubt.)

You can take the Browns' data and adjust the figures for every category and for every year, either by changing the growth percentages to automatically fill in the spreadsheet cells, or by entering whatever numbers you would like in each cell, one-by-one.

Table A-4: Tax Tables

This worksheet shows the federal tax tables used for all tax calculations. The first two tables—*Estate Tax Rate* and *Unified Credit*—have been taken straight from the IRS manual. The third one, *Retirement Plan Distribution Percentage at Given Age,* addresses mandated distribution from your qualified retirement plans. That table only offers a "typical" example, useful as a general rule of thumb. If you are really serious here, ask your accountant to calculate the table for your specific situation.

Main Program (MAIN)

This is the main worksheet for the Family Financial Program. It prints out as sixteen legal-sized pages. The Summary Sheets (two graphs and a table) are also on this worksheet. We don't include a copy of the sixteen pages in this book; you can get it from the Internet download.

If you are really intrigued, print out the sixteen pages, tape them into doubles, and lay them out on a table. You will be able to follow every detail and calculation that leads to the sample results given in this book.

Table A-1: Starting Page

**Enter data on this sheet
in dotted line boxes**

To Select Family:

Enter Family Number: (1, 2, 3, 4, 5 OR 6)

HERE ----> :·······2·······: **Brown** **FAMILY**

1	Allen
2	Brown
3	Clark
4	Drake
5	Emory
6	Finch

To Run With Both Gifting Options:

Enter: CTRL-SHFT-G

To Run With Single Gifting Option:

(1) Enter Gifting Option Number: (1 OR 2)

HERE ----> :·······1·······: **WITH GIFTING**

1	WITH GIFTING
2	WITHOUT GIFTING

(2) Enter: CTRL-SHFT-E

Table A-2: *Starting Data for Six Families*

Enter data on this sheet in dotted line boxes

FAMILY		F CURRENT RUN	G	H	I	J	K	L
			1	2	3	4	5	6
NUMBER	6	2	Allen	Brown	Clark	Drake	Emory	Finch
NAME	7	Brown	COMFORTABLE	VERY	RICH	SOLID	RICH	GREAT
				COMFORTABLE		CITIZENS		POTENTIAL
AGE AND TIME FACTORS								
CURENT YEAR	11	2000	2000	2000	2000	2000	2000	2000
STARTING AGE (JANUARY 1)	12	60	60	60	60	60	70	45
AGE AT DEATH		90	90	90	90	90	100	75
NET WORTH ACCOUNTS								
(A) INVESTMENTS - OTHER	16	800,000	400,000	800,000	2,000,000	300,000	2,000,000	50,000
GROWTH	17	7.0%	7.0%	7.0%	7.0%	0.0%	0.0%	10.0%
INCOME	18	2.0%	2.0%	2.0%	2.0%	6.0%	6.0%	2.0%
TOTAL RETURN		9.0%	9.0%	9.0%	9.0%	6.0%	6.0%	12.0%
(B1) RET ACCTS (DISTRIBUTED)			0	0	0	0	0	0
GROWTH	22	7.0%	7.0%	7.0%	7.0%	0.0%	0.0%	10.0%
INCOME	23	2.0%	2.0%	2.0%	2.0%	6.0%	6.0%	2.0%
TOTAL RETURN		9.0%	9.0%	9.0%	9.0%	6.0%	6.0%	12.0%
(B2) RET ACCTS (UNDISTRIBUTED)	26	700,000	400,000	700,000	1,500,000	300,000	1,500,000	50,000
GROWTH AND INCOME	27	9.0%	9.0%	9.0%	9.0%	6.0%	6.0%	12.0%
(C) REAL ESTATE EQUITY	29	300,000	200,000	300,000	300,000	200,000	300,000	50,000
GROWTH	30	3.0%	3.0%	3.0%	3.0%	2.0%	2.0%	2.0%
(D) LIFE INSURANCE AMOUNT	32	700,000	500,000	700,000	1,200,000	400,000	1,200,000	100,000
TOTAL NET WORTH (IN ESTATE)		2,500,000	1,500,000	2,500,000	5,000,000	1,200,000	5,000,000	250,000
"ENOUGH"	37	2,000,000	1,000,000	2,000,000	2,500,000	850,000	2,500,000	3,000,000
RATE OF INCREASE	38	2.0%	2.0%	2.0%	2.0%	2.0%	2.0%	2.0%
MINIMUM TO BE RETAINED IN (A) INVEST		600,000	400,000	600,000	800,000	300,000	800,000	50,000
OK GROWTH	41	3.0%	3.0%	3.0%	3.0%	3.0%	3.0%	3.0%
ANTICIPATED INHERITANCE OR DEPOSIT		500,000	250,000	500,000	1,000,000	100,000	500,000	5,000,000
YEAR RECEIVED	44	2007	2007	2007	2007	2007	2007	2005
TAX RATES								
INCOME TAX - FEDERAL			25.0%	30.0%	35.0%	20.0%	30.0%	30.0%
INCOME TAX - STATE			3.0%	3.0%	3.0%	3.0%	3.0%	3.0%
INCOME TAX - TOTAL	49	33.0%	28.0%	33.0%	38.0%	23.0%	33.0%	33.0%
INCOME TAX - RET ACCTS	50	40.0%	40.0%	40.0%	40.0%	40.0%	40.0%	40.0%
CAPITAL GAINS TAX - TOTAL	51	20.0%	20.0%	20.0%	20.0%	20.0%	20.0%	20.0%
% OF S/S SUBJECT TO INCM TAX	52	85.0%	85.0%	85.0%	85.0%	85.0%	85.0%	85.0%
OTHER								
ANNUAL INFLATION - DEFAULT	54	3.0%	3.0%	3.0%	3.0%	3.0%	3.0%	3.0%
CAPITAL SOLD (TYPICAL ANNUAL)		10.0%	10.0%	10.0%	10.0%	10.0%	10.0%	10.0%
CAP GNS REALIZED ON TYP CAP SALE		40.0%	40.0%	40.0%	40.0%	40.0%	40.0%	40.0%

Table A-3: Lifetime Data

Data from the Brown Family Data Sheet
2

Do not enter data on this sheet

| | | Other Income | | | S/S | Annual Gifting | | | | | | Living |
| | | | | (F) | (E) | | | Charity Gifting | | Total | Total | |
Year	Age	Salary and Wages	Misc Income	Pension	Total Other Income	Social Sec	Family Gifting	Stock	Cash	Total Charity Gifting	Total Gifting	Living Expenses
Annual Growth		5.0%	3.0%			3.0%	4.0%	4.0%	4.0%			2.0%
2000	60	60,000	15,000	15,000	90,000		20,000	25,000	3,000	28,000	48,000	90,000
2001	61	50,000	15,750	15,450	81,200		20,800	26,000	3,120	29,120	49,920	91,800
2002	62	40,000	16,538	15,914	72,451	18,000	21,632	27,040	3,245	30,285	51,917	93,636
2003	63	30,000	17,364	16,391	63,755	18,540	22,497	28,122	3,375	31,496	53,993	95,509
2004	64	20,000	18,233	16,883	55,115	19,096	23,397	29,246	3,510	32,756	56,153	97,419
2005	65	10,000	19,144	17,389	46,533	19,669	24,333	30,416	3,650	34,066	58,399	99,367
2006	66		20,101	17,911	38,012	20,259	25,306	31,633	3,796	35,429	60,735	101,355
2007	67		21,107	18,448	39,555	20,867	26,319	32,898	3,948	36,846	63,165	103,382
2008	68		22,162	19,002	41,163	21,493	27,371	34,214	4,106	38,320	65,691	105,449
2009	69		23,270	19,572	42,842	22,138	28,466	35,583	4,270	39,853	68,319	107,558
2010	70		24,433	20,159	44,592	22,802	29,605	37,006	4,441	41,447	71,052	109,709
2011	71		25,655	20,764	46,419	23,486	30,789	38,486	4,618	43,105	73,894	111,904
2012	72		26,938	21,386	48,324	24,190	32,021	40,026	4,803	44,829	76,850	114,142
2013	73		28,285	22,028	50,313	24,916	33,301	41,627	4,995	46,622	79,924	116,425
2014	74		29,699	22,689	52,388	25,664	34,634	43,292	5,195	48,487	83,120	118,753
2015	75		31,184	23,370	54,553	26,434	36,019	45,024	5,403	50,426	86,445	121,128
2016	76		32,743	24,071	56,814	27,227	37,460	46,825	5,619	52,443	89,903	123,551
2017	77		34,380	24,793	59,173	28,043	38,958	48,698	5,844	54,541	93,499	126,022
2018	78		36,099	25,536	61,636	28,885	40,516	50,645	6,077	56,723	97,239	128,542
2019	79		37,904	26,303	64,207	29,751	42,137	52,671	6,321	58,992	101,129	131,113
2020	80		39,799	27,092	66,891	30,644	43,822	54,778	6,573	61,351	105,174	133,735
2021	81		41,789	27,904	69,694	31,563	45,575	56,969	6,836	63,806	109,381	136,410
2022	82		43,879	28,742	72,620	32,510	47,398	59,248	7,110	66,358	113,756	139,138
2023	83		46,073	29,604	75,677	33,485	49,294	61,618	7,394	69,012	118,306	141,921
2024	84		48,376	30,492	78,868	34,490	51,266	64,083	7,690	71,773	123,039	144,759
2025	85		50,795	31,407	82,202	35,525	53,317	66,646	7,998	74,643	127,960	147,655
2026	86		53,335	32,349	85,684	36,590	55,449	69,312	8,317	77,629	133,079	150,608
2027	87		56,002	33,319	89,321	37,688	57,667	72,084	8,650	80,734	138,402	153,620
2028	88		58,802	34,319	93,121	38,819	59,974	74,968	8,996	83,964	143,938	156,692
2029	89		61,742	35,348	97,091	39,983	62,373	77,966	9,356	87,322	149,695	159,826
47		210,000	996,583	713,631	1,920,214	772,757	1,121,699	1,402,123	168,255	1,570,378	2,692,077	3,651,127

RANGE NAME IS "LIFEDATA"

Table A-4: Tax Tables

Do not enter data on this sheet

A	B	C		E	F	G	H	I		K	L
ESTATE TAX				UNIFIED CREDIT						RETIREMENT PLAN	
AT GIVEN TAX BRACKET AND GIVEN TAXABLE INCOME				YEAR	UNIFIED CREDIT FOR ONE	UNIFIED CREDIT FOR TWO	ESTATE TAX ALLOWANCE			DISTRIBUTION % AT GIVEN AGE	
(A) AMOUNT EXCEEDED	(C) TAX ON (A)	(D) TAX RATE ON AMT OVER (A)					FOR ONE PERSON	FOR TWO PEOPLE		AGE	DISTRIB
500,000	155,800	37.0%		1997	192,800	385,600	600,000	1,200,000	16	71	4.7%
750,000	248,300	39.0%		1998	202,050	404,100	625,000	1,250,000	17	72	4.9%
1,000,000	345,800	41.0%		1999	211,300	422,600	650,000	1,300,000	18	73	5.1%
1,250,000	448,300	43.0%		2000	220,550	441,100	675,000	1,350,000	19	74	5.4%
1,500,000	555,800	45.0%		2001	220,550	441,100	675,000	1,350,000	20	75	5.7%
2,000,000	780,800	49.0%		2002	229,800	459,600	700,000	1,400,000	21	76	6.1%
2,500,000	1,025,800	53.0%		2003	229,800	459,600	700,000	1,400,000	22	77	6.5%
3,000,000	1,290,800	55.0%		2004	287,300	574,600	850,000	1,700,000	23	78	6.9%
				2005	326,300	652,600	950,000	1,900,000	24	79	7.4%
				2006	345,800	691,600	1,000,000	2,000,000	25	80	8.0%
				>2006	345,800	691,600	1,000,000	2,000,000	26	81	8.7%
									27	82	9.5%
									28	83	10.5%
MAXIMUM TAX DEDUCTIBILITY LIMITATIONS - CHARITIBLE GIFTING									29	84	11.8%
STOCK GIFTING (MARKET VALUE), PERCENT OF AGI		30.0%							30	85	14.4%
TOTAL GIFTING, PERCENT OF AGI		50.0%							31	86	15.4%
									32	87	18.2%
									33	88	22.2%
									34	89	28.6%
									35	90	40.0%
									36	91	66.7%
									37	92	100.0%
									38	93	0.0%
* TYPICAL DISTRIBUTION REQUIREMENTS. SEE YOUR PROFESSIONAL ADVISOR									39	94	0.0%
FOR CACULATIONS SPECIFIC TO YOUR SITUATION.									40	95	0.0%
									41	96	0.0%
									42	97	0.0%
									43	98	0.0%
									44	99	0.0%
									45	100	0.0%

Appendix B
Starting Data

Table B-1: Allen Family Data

Enter Data on this Sheet in Dotted Line Boxes

Year	Age	Salary and Wages	Misc Income	Pension	Total Other Income	Social Security	Family Gifting	Charity Gifting Stock	Charity Gifting Cash	Total Charity Gifting	Total Gifting	Living Expenses
Annual Growth		5.0%	3.0%			3.0%	1.0%	1.0%	1.0%			2.0%
2000	60	25,000	10,000	15,000	50,000	0	10,000	8,000	2,000	10,000	20,000	75,000
2001	61	25,000	10,500	15,450	50,950	0	10,100	8,080	2,020	10,100	20,200	76,500
2002	62	25,000	11,025	15,914	51,939	18,000	10,201	8,161	2,040	10,201	20,402	78,030
2003	63	25,000	11,576	16,391	52,967	18,540	10,303	8,242	2,061	10,303	20,606	79,591
2004	64	25,000	12,155	16,883	54,038	19,096	10,406	8,325	2,081	10,406	20,812	81,182
2005	65	25,000	12,763	17,389	55,152	19,669	10,510	8,408	2,102	10,510	21,020	82,806
2006	66		13,401	17,911	31,312	20,259	10,615	8,492	2,123	10,615	21,230	84,462
2007	67		14,071	18,448	32,519	20,867	10,721	8,577	2,144	10,721	21,443	86,151
2008	68		14,775	19,002	33,776	21,493	10,829	8,663	2,166	10,829	21,657	87,874
2009	69		15,513	19,572	35,085	22,138	10,937	8,749	2,187	10,937	21,874	89,632
2010	70		16,289	20,159	36,448	22,802	11,046	8,837	2,209	11,046	22,092	91,425
2011	71		17,103	20,764	37,867	23,486	11,157	8,925	2,231	11,157	22,313	93,253
2012	72		17,959	21,386	39,345	24,190	11,268	9,015	2,254	11,268	22,537	95,118
2013	73		18,856	22,028	40,884	24,916	11,381	9,105	2,276	11,381	22,762	97,020
2014	74		19,799	22,689	42,488	25,664	11,495	9,196	2,299	11,495	22,989	98,961
2015	75		20,789	23,370	44,159	26,434	11,610	9,288	2,322	11,610	23,219	100,940
2016	76		21,829	24,071	45,899	27,227	11,726	9,381	2,345	11,726	23,452	102,959
2017	77		22,920	24,793	47,713	28,043	11,843	9,474	2,369	11,843	23,686	105,018
2018	78		24,066	25,536	49,603	28,885	11,961	9,569	2,392	11,961	23,923	107,118
2019	79		25,270	26,303	51,572	29,751	12,081	9,665	2,416	12,081	24,162	109,261
2020	80		26,533	27,092	53,625	30,644	12,202	9,762	2,440	12,202	24,404	111,446
2021	81		27,860	27,904	55,764	31,563	12,324	9,859	2,465	12,324	24,648	113,675
2022	82		29,253	28,742	57,994	32,510	12,447	9,958	2,489	12,447	24,894	115,948
2023	83		30,715	29,604	60,319	33,485	12,572	10,057	2,514	12,572	25,143	118,267
2024	84		32,251	30,492	62,743	34,490	12,697	10,158	2,539	12,697	25,395	120,633
2025	85		33,864	31,407	65,270	35,525	12,824	10,259	2,565	12,824	25,649	123,045
2026	86		35,557	32,349	67,906	36,590	12,953	10,362	2,591	12,953	25,905	125,506
2027	87		37,335	33,319	70,654	37,688	13,082	10,466	2,616	13,082	26,164	128,016
2028	88		39,201	34,319	73,520	38,819	13,213	10,570	2,643	13,213	26,426	130,577
2029	89		41,161	35,348	76,510	39,983	13,345	10,676	2,669	13,345	26,690	133,188
		150,000	**664,388**	**713,631**	**1,528,020**	**772,757**	**347,849**	**278,279**	**69,570**	**347,849**	**695,698**	**3,042,606**

Table B-2: Brown Family Data

Enter Data on this Sheet in Dotted Line Boxes

RUN NUMBER		Other Income				S/S	Annual Gifting						Living
		Salary and Wages	Misc Income	Pension	Total Other Income	Social Sec	Family Gifting	Charity Gifting Stock	Charity Gifting Cash	Total Charity Gifting	Total Gifting		Living Expenses
Annual Growth		5.0%	3.0%			3.0%	4.0%	4.0%	4.0%				2.0%
Year	Age												
2000	60	60,000	15,000	15,000	90,000		20,000	25,000	3,000	28,000	48,000		90,000
2001	61	50,000	15,750	15,450	81,200		20,800	26,000	3,120	29,120	49,920		91,800
2002	62	40,000	16,538	15,914	72,451	18,000	21,632	27,040	3,245	30,285	51,917		93,636
2003	63	30,000	17,364	16,391	63,755	18,540	22,497	28,122	3,375	31,496	53,993		95,509
2004	64	20,000	18,233	16,883	55,115	19,096	23,397	29,246	3,510	32,756	56,153		97,419
2005	65	10,000	19,144	17,389	46,533	19,669	24,333	30,416	3,650	34,066	58,399		99,367
2006	66		20,101	17,911	38,012	20,259	25,306	31,633	3,796	35,429	60,735		101,355
2007	67		21,107	18,448	39,555	20,867	26,319	32,898	3,948	36,846	63,165		103,382
2008	68		22,162	19,002	41,163	21,493	27,371	34,214	4,106	38,320	65,691		105,449
2009	69		23,270	19,572	42,842	22,138	28,466	35,583	4,270	39,853	68,319		107,558
2010	70		24,433	20,159	44,592	22,802	29,605	37,006	4,441	41,447	71,052		109,709
2011	71		25,655	20,764	46,419	23,486	30,789	38,486	4,618	43,105	73,894		111,904
2012	72		26,938	21,386	48,324	24,190	32,021	40,026	4,803	44,829	76,850		114,142
2013	73		28,285	22,028	50,313	24,916	33,301	41,627	4,995	46,622	79,924		116,425
2014	74		29,699	22,689	52,388	25,664	34,634	43,292	5,195	48,487	83,120		118,753
2015	75		31,184	23,370	54,553	26,434	36,019	45,024	5,403	50,426	86,445		121,128
2016	76		32,743	24,071	56,814	27,227	37,460	46,825	5,619	52,443	89,903		123,551
2017	77		34,380	24,793	59,173	28,043	38,958	48,698	5,844	54,541	93,499		126,022
2018	78		36,099	25,536	61,636	28,885	40,516	50,645	6,077	56,723	97,239		128,542
2019	79		37,904	26,303	64,207	29,751	42,137	52,671	6,321	58,992	101,129		131,113
2020	80		39,799	27,092	66,891	30,644	43,822	54,778	6,573	61,351	105,174		133,735
2021	81		41,789	27,904	69,694	31,563	45,575	56,969	6,836	63,806	109,381		136,410
2022	82		43,879	28,742	72,620	32,510	47,398	59,248	7,110	66,358	113,756		139,138
2023	83		46,073	29,604	75,677	33,485	49,294	61,618	7,394	69,012	118,306		141,921
2024	84		48,376	30,492	78,868	34,490	51,266	64,083	7,690	71,773	123,039		144,759
2025	85		50,795	31,407	82,202	35,525	53,317	66,646	7,998	74,643	127,960		147,655
2026	86		53,335	32,349	85,684	36,590	55,449	69,312	8,317	77,629	133,079		150,608
2027	87		56,002	33,319	89,321	37,688	57,667	72,084	8,650	80,734	138,402		153,620
2028	88		58,802	34,319	93,121	38,819	59,974	74,968	8,996	83,964	143,938		156,692
2029	89		61,742	35,348	97,091	39,983	62,373	77,966	9,356	87,322	149,695		159,826
		210,000	996,583	713,631	1,920,214	772,757	1,121,699	1,402,123	168,255	1,570,378	2,692,077		3,651,127

Table B-3: Clark Family Data

Enter Data on this Sheet in Dotted Line Boxes

Year	Age	Other Income				S/S	Annual Gifting						Living
		Salary and Wages	Misc Income	Pension	Total Other Income	Social Sec	Family Gifting	Charity Gifting Stock	Charity Gifting Cash	Total Charity Gifting	Total Gifting	Living Expenses
Annual Growth		5.0%	3.0%			3.0%	4.0%	4.0%	4.0%			2.0%
2000	60	35,000	30,000	30,000	95,000		60,000	65,000	5,000	70,000	130,000	150,000
2001	61	35,000	31,500	30,900	97,400		62,400	67,600	5,200	72,800	135,200	153,000
2002	62	35,000	33,075	31,827	99,902	18,000	64,896	70,304	5,408	75,712	140,608	156,060
2003	63	35,000	34,729	32,782	102,511	18,540	67,492	73,116	5,624	78,740	146,232	159,181
2004	64	35,000	36,465	33,765	105,230	19,096	70,192	76,041	5,849	81,890	152,082	162,365
2005	65	35,000	38,288	34,778	108,067	19,669	72,999	79,082	6,083	85,166	158,165	165,612
2006	66		40,203	35,822	76,024	20,259	75,919	82,246	6,327	88,572	164,491	168,924
2007	67		42,213	36,896	79,109	20,867	78,956	85,536	6,580	92,115	171,071	172,303
2008	68		44,324	38,003	82,327	21,493	82,114	88,957	6,843	95,800	177,914	175,749
2009	69		46,540	39,143	85,683	22,138	85,399	92,515	7,117	99,632	185,031	179,264
2010	70		48,867	40,317	89,184	22,802	88,815	96,216	7,401	103,617	192,432	182,849
2011	71		51,310	41,527	92,837	23,486	92,367	100,065	7,697	107,762	200,129	186,506
2012	72		53,876	42,773	96,649	24,190	96,062	104,067	8,005	112,072	208,134	190,236
2013	73		56,569	44,056	100,625	24,916	99,904	108,230	8,325	116,555	216,460	194,041
2014	74		59,398	45,378	104,776	25,664	103,901	112,559	8,658	121,217	225,118	197,922
2015	75		62,368	46,739	109,107	26,434	108,057	117,061	9,005	126,066	234,123	201,880
2016	76		65,486	48,141	113,627	27,227	112,379	121,744	9,365	131,109	243,488	205,918
2017	77		68,761	49,585	118,346	28,043	116,874	126,614	9,740	136,353	253,227	210,036
2018	78		72,199	51,073	123,272	28,885	121,549	131,678	10,129	141,807	263,356	214,237
2019	79		75,809	52,605	128,414	29,751	126,411	136,945	10,534	147,479	273,890	218,522
2020	80		79,599	54,183	133,782	30,644	131,467	142,423	10,956	153,379	284,846	222,892
2021	81		83,579	55,809	139,388	31,563	136,726	148,120	11,394	159,514	296,240	227,350
2022	82		87,758	57,483	145,241	32,510	142,195	154,045	11,850	165,894	308,089	231,897
2023	83		92,146	59,208	151,353	33,485	147,883	160,207	12,324	172,530	320,413	236,535
2024	84		96,753	60,984	157,737	34,490	153,798	166,615	12,817	179,431	333,230	241,266
2025	85		101,591	62,813	164,404	35,525	159,950	173,279	13,329	186,609	346,559	246,091
2026	86		106,670	64,698	171,368	36,590	166,348	180,211	13,862	194,073	360,421	251,013
2027	87		112,004	66,639	178,642	37,688	173,002	187,419	14,417	201,836	374,838	256,033
2028	88		117,604	68,638	186,242	38,819	179,922	194,916	14,994	209,909	389,831	261,154
2029	89		123,484	70,697	194,181	39,983	187,119	202,712	15,593	218,306	405,425	266,377
		210,000	1,993,165	1,427,262	3,630,428	772,757	3,365,096	3,645,521	280,425	3,925,946	7,291,042	6,085,212

Table B-4: Drake Family Data

Enter Data on this Sheet in Dotted Line Boxes

		Other Income				S/S	Annual Gifting						Living
		Salary and Wages	Misc Income	Pension	Total Other Income	Social Sec	Family Gifting	Charity Gifting Stock	Charity Gifting Cash	Total Charity Gifting	Total Gifting		Living Expenses
Annual Growth		5.0%	3.0%			3.0%	5.0%	5.0%	5.0%				2.0%
Year	**Age**												
2000	60	20,000	10,000	10,000	40,000		2,000	1,000	1,000	2,000	4,000		50,000
2001	61	20,000	10,500	10,300	40,800		2,100	1,050	1,050	2,100	4,200		51,000
2002	62	20,000	11,025	10,609	41,634	18,000	2,205	1,103	1,103	2,205	4,410		52,020
2003	63	20,000	11,576	10,927	42,504	18,540	2,315	1,158	1,158	2,315	4,631		53,060
2004	64	20,000	12,155	11,255	43,410	19,096	2,431	1,216	1,216	2,431	4,862		54,122
2005	65	20,000	12,763	11,593	44,356	19,669	2,553	1,276	1,276	2,553	5,105		55,204
2006	66	20,000	13,401	11,941	45,341	20,259	2,680	1,340	1,340	2,680	5,360		56,308
2007	67		14,071	12,299	26,370	20,867	2,814	1,407	1,407	2,814	5,628		57,434
2008	68		14,775	12,668	27,442	21,493	2,955	1,477	1,477	2,955	5,910		58,583
2009	69		15,513	13,048	28,561	22,138	3,103	1,551	1,551	3,103	6,205		59,755
2010	70		16,289	13,439	29,728	22,802	3,258	1,629	1,629	3,258	6,516		60,950
2011	71		17,103	13,842	30,946	23,486	3,421	1,710	1,710	3,421	6,841		62,169
2012	72		17,959	14,258	32,216	24,190	3,592	1,796	1,796	3,592	7,183		63,412
2013	73		18,856	14,685	33,542	24,916	3,771	1,886	1,886	3,771	7,543		64,680
2014	74		19,799	15,126	34,925	25,664	3,960	1,980	1,980	3,960	7,920		65,974
2015	75		20,789	15,580	36,369	26,434	4,158	2,079	2,079	4,158	8,316		67,293
2016	76		21,829	16,047	37,876	27,227	4,366	2,183	2,183	4,366	8,731		68,639
2017	77		22,920	16,528	39,449	28,043	4,584	2,292	2,292	4,584	9,168		70,012
2018	78		24,066	17,024	41,091	28,885	4,813	2,407	2,407	4,813	9,626		71,412
2019	79		25,270	17,535	42,805	29,751	5,054	2,527	2,527	5,054	10,108		72,841
2020	80		26,533	18,061	44,594	30,644	5,307	2,653	2,653	5,307	10,613		74,297
2021	81		27,860	18,603	46,463	31,563	5,572	2,786	2,786	5,572	11,144		75,783
2022	82		29,253	19,161	48,414	32,510	5,851	2,925	2,925	5,851	11,701		77,299
2023	83		30,715	19,736	50,451	33,485	6,143	3,072	3,072	6,143	12,286		78,845
2024	84		32,251	20,328	52,579	34,490	6,450	3,225	3,225	6,450	12,900		80,422
2025	85		33,864	20,938	54,801	35,525	6,773	3,386	3,386	6,773	13,545		82,030
2026	86		35,557	21,566	57,123	36,590	7,111	3,556	3,556	7,111	14,223		83,671
2027	87		37,335	22,213	59,547	37,688	7,467	3,733	3,733	7,467	14,934		85,344
2028	88		39,201	22,879	62,081	38,819	7,840	3,920	3,920	7,840	15,681		87,051
2029	89		41,161	23,566	64,727	39,983	8,232	4,116	4,116	8,232	16,465		88,792
		140,000	664,388	475,754	1,280,143	772,757	132,878	66,439	66,439	132,878	265,755		2,028,404

Table B-5: Emory Family Data

Enter Data on this Sheet in Dotted Line Boxes

Year	Age		Salary and Wages	Misc Income	Pension	Total Other Income	Social Sec	Family Gifting	Charity Gifting Stock	Charity Gifting Cash	Total Charity Gifting	Total Gifting	Living Expenses
			Other Income				**S/S**	**Annual Gifting**					**Living**
Annual Growth			5.0%	3.0%			3.0%	4.0%	4.0%	4.0%			2.0%
2000	70	0	15,000	20,000	35,000		19,957	25,000	20,000	3,000	23,000	48,000	110,000
2001	71		15,750	20,600	36,350		20,556	26,000	20,800	3,120	23,920	49,920	112,200
2002	72		16,538	21,218	37,756		21,172	27,040	21,632	3,245	24,877	51,917	114,444
2003	73		17,364	21,855	39,219		21,808	28,122	22,497	3,375	25,872	53,993	116,733
2004	74		18,233	22,510	40,743		22,462	29,246	23,397	3,510	26,907	56,153	119,068
2005	75		19,144	23,185	42,330		23,136	30,416	24,333	3,650	27,983	58,399	121,449
2006	76		20,101	23,881	43,982		23,830	31,633	25,306	3,796	29,102	60,735	123,878
2007	77		21,107	24,597	45,704		24,545	32,898	26,319	3,948	30,266	63,165	126,355
2008	78		22,162	25,335	47,497		25,281	34,214	27,371	4,106	31,477	65,691	128,883
2009	79		23,270	26,095	49,365		26,039	35,583	28,466	4,270	32,736	68,319	131,460
2010	80		24,433	26,878	51,312		26,821	37,006	29,605	4,441	34,046	71,052	134,089
2011	81		25,655	27,685	53,340		27,625	38,486	30,789	4,618	35,407	73,894	136,771
2012	82		26,938	28,515	55,453		28,454	40,026	32,021	4,803	36,824	76,850	139,507
2013	83		28,285	29,371	57,655		29,308	41,627	33,301	4,995	38,297	79,924	142,297
2014	84		29,699	30,252	59,951		30,187	43,292	34,634	5,195	39,829	83,120	145,143
2015	85		31,184	31,159	62,343		31,092	45,024	36,019	5,403	41,422	86,445	148,046
2016	86		32,743	32,094	64,837		32,025	46,825	37,460	5,619	43,079	89,903	151,006
2017	87		34,380	33,057	67,437		32,986	48,698	38,958	5,844	44,802	93,499	154,027
2018	88		36,099	34,049	70,148		33,975	50,645	40,516	6,077	46,594	97,239	157,107
2019	89		37,904	35,070	72,974		34,995	52,671	42,137	6,321	48,458	101,129	160,249
2020	90		39,799	36,122	75,922		36,045	54,778	43,822	6,573	50,396	105,174	163,454
2021	91		41,789	37,206	78,995		37,126	56,969	45,575	6,836	52,412	109,381	166,723
2022	92		43,879	38,322	82,201		38,240	59,248	47,398	7,110	54,508	113,756	170,058
2023	93		46,073	39,472	85,545		39,387	61,618	49,294	7,394	56,688	118,306	173,459
2024	94		48,376	40,656	89,032		40,568	64,083	51,266	7,690	58,956	123,039	176,928
2025	95		50,795	41,876	92,671		41,786	66,646	53,317	7,998	61,314	127,960	180,467
2026	96		53,335	43,132	96,467		43,039	69,312	55,449	8,317	63,767	133,079	184,076
2027	97		56,002	44,426	100,428		44,330	72,084	57,667	8,650	66,317	138,402	187,758
2028	98		58,802	45,759	104,560		45,660	74,968	59,974	8,996	68,970	143,938	191,513
2029	99		61,742	47,131	108,873		47,030	77,966	62,373	9,356	71,729	149,695	195,343
		0	996,583	951,508	1,948,091		949,463	1,402,123	1,121,699	168,255	1,289,954	2,692,077	4,462,489

Table B-6: Finch Family Data

Enter Data on this Sheet in Dotted Line Boxes

Year	Age	Salary and Wages	Misc Income	Pension	Total Other Income	Social Sec	Family Gifting	Charity Gifting Stock	Charity Gifting Cash	Total Charity Gifting	Total Gifting	Living Expenses
Annual Growth		3.0%	3.0%			3.0%	6.0%	6.0%	6.0%			2.0%
2000	45	60,000	15,000		75,000		1,000	1,000	1,000	2,000	3,000	55,000
2001	46	60,000	15,450		75,450		1,060	1,060	1,060	2,120	3,180	56,100
2002	47	60,000	15,914		75,914		1,124	1,124	1,124	2,247	3,371	57,222
2003	48	60,000	16,391		76,391		1,191	1,191	1,191	2,382	3,573	58,366
2004	49	60,000	16,883		76,883		1,262	1,262	1,262	2,525	3,787	59,534
2005	50	60,000	17,389		77,389		1,338	1,338	1,338	2,676	4,015	60,724
2006	51	60,000	17,911		77,911		1,419	1,419	1,419	2,837	4,256	150,000
2007	52	60,000	18,448		78,448		100,000	70,000	5,000	75,000	175,000	153,000
2008	53	60,000	19,002		79,002		106,000	74,200	5,300	79,500	185,500	156,060
2009	54	60,000	19,572		79,572		112,360	78,652	5,618	84,270	196,630	159,181
2010	55	60,000	20,159		80,159		119,102	83,371	5,955	89,326	208,428	162,365
2011	56	60,000	20,764		80,764		126,248	88,373	6,312	94,686	220,933	165,612
2012	57	60,000	21,386		81,386		133,823	93,676	6,691	100,367	234,189	168,924
2013	58	60,000	22,028		82,028		141,852	99,296	7,093	106,389	248,241	172,303
2014	59	60,000	22,689		82,689		150,363	105,254	7,518	112,772	263,135	175,749
2015	60	60,000	23,370	15,000	98,370		159,385	500,000	7,969	507,969	667,354	179,264
2016	61		24,071	15,450	39,521		168,948	530,000	8,447	538,447	707,395	182,849
2017	62		24,793	15,914	40,706	35,816	179,085	561,800	8,954	570,754	749,839	186,506
2018	63		25,536	16,391	41,927	36,890	189,830	595,508	9,491	604,999	794,829	190,236
2019	64		26,303	16,883	43,185	37,997	201,220	631,238	10,061	641,299	842,519	194,041
2020	65		27,092	17,389	44,481	39,137	213,293	669,113	10,665	679,777	893,070	197,922
2021	66		27,904	17,911	45,815	40,311	226,090	709,260	11,305	720,564	946,654	201,880
2022	67		28,742	18,448	47,190	41,521	239,656	751,815	11,983	763,798	1,003,454	205,918
2023	68		29,604	19,002	48,605	42,766	254,035	796,924	12,702	809,626	1,063,661	210,036
2024	69		30,492	19,572	50,064	44,049	269,277	844,739	13,464	858,203	1,127,481	214,237
2025	70		31,407	20,159	51,565	45,371	285,434	895,424	14,272	909,696	1,195,129	218,522
2026	71		32,349	20,764	53,112	46,732	302,560	949,149	15,128	964,277	1,266,837	222,892
2027	72		33,319	21,386	54,706	48,134	320,714	1,006,098	16,036	1,022,134	1,342,847	227,350
2028	73		34,319	22,028	56,347	49,578	339,956	1,066,464	16,998	1,083,462	1,423,418	231,897
2029	74		35,348	22,689	58,037	51,065	360,354	1,130,452	18,018	1,148,470	1,508,823	236,535
		960,000	713,631	278,984	1,952,615	559,367	4,707,977	12,339,202	243,373	12,582,575	17,290,551	4,910,226

Appendix C
Six Family's Net Worth

Figure C-1: Net Worth for Allen Family

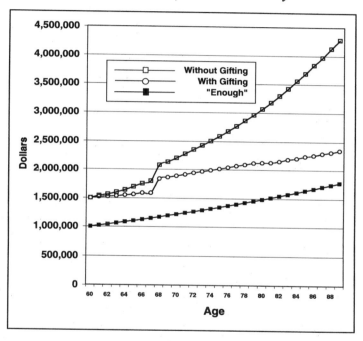

Chart - Net Worth		
	Starting Year	Ending Year
Without Gifting	1,500,000	4,284,911
With Gifting	1,500,000	2,346,970
Enough	1,000,000	1,775,845

Figure C-2: Net Worth for Brown Family

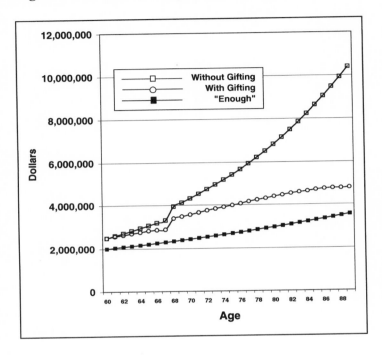

Chart - Net Worth		
	Starting Year	Ending Year
Without Gifting	2,500,000	10,393,275
With Gifting	2,500,000	4,794,037
Enough	2,000,000	3,551,689

Figure C-3: Net Worth for the Clark Family

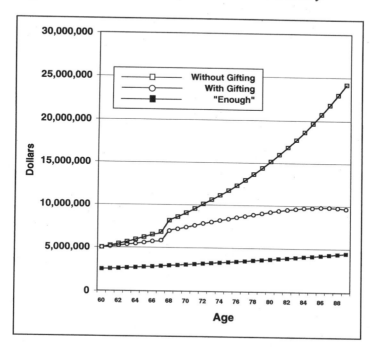

Chart - Net Worth		
	Starting Year	Ending Year
Without Gifting	5,000,000	24,160,944
With Gifting	5,000,000	9,658,547
Enough	2,500,000	4,439,612

Figure C-4: Net Worth for the Drake Family

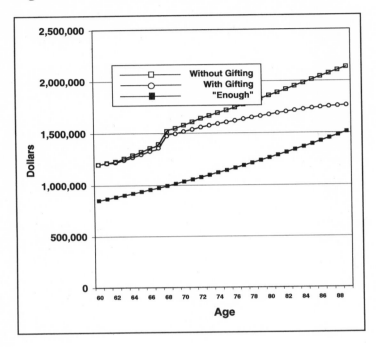

Chart - Net Worth		
	Starting Year	Ending Year
Without Gifting	1,200,000	2,134,285
With Gifting	1,200,000	1,761,645
Enough	850,000	1,509,468

Figure C-5: Net Worth for the Emory Family

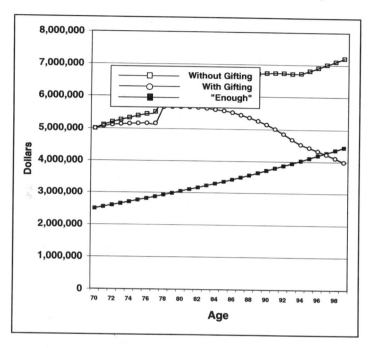

Chart - Net Worth		
	Starting Year	Ending Year
Without Gifting	5,000,000	7,205,323
With Gifting	5,000,000	3,988,003
Enough	2,500,000	4,439,612

Figure C-6: Net Worth for the Finch Family

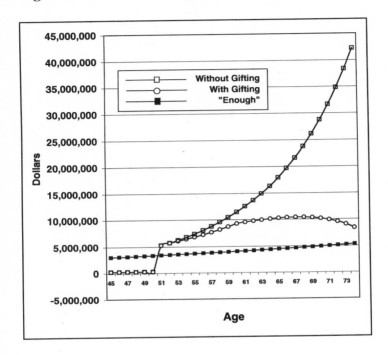

Chart - Net Worth		
	Starting Year	Ending Year
Without Gifting	250,000	42,249,234
With Gifting	250,000	8,410,475
Enough	3,000,000	5,327,534

Appendix D
Six Family's Total Gifting

Figure D-1: Total Gifting for Allen Family

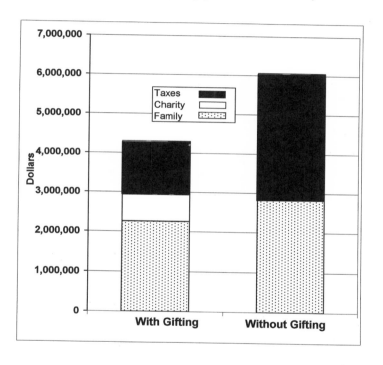

Chart - Lifetime Giving		
	With Gifting	Without Gifting
Taxes	1,359,237	3,226,506
Charity	685,611	0
Family	2,250,033	2,831,973
Totals	4,294,880	6,058,479

Figure D-2: Total Gifting for Brown Family

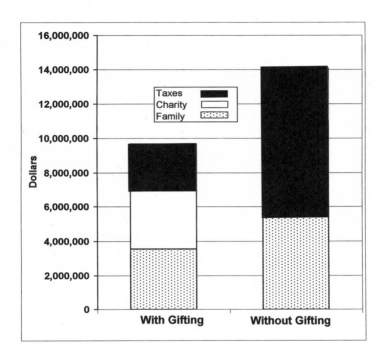

Chart - Lifetime Giving		
	With Gifting	Without Gifting
Taxes	2,747,788	8,662,377
Charity	3,383,465	0
Family	3,545,610	5,413,303
Totals	9,676,863	14,075,681

Figure D-3: Total Gifting for Clark Family

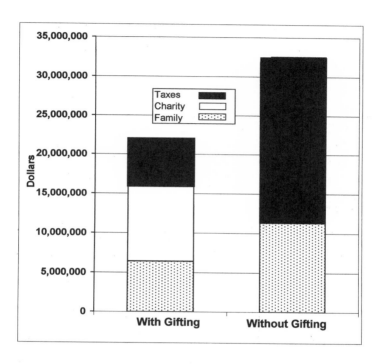

Chart - Lifetime Giving		
	With Gifting	Without Gifting
Taxes	6,048,643	21,207,912
Charity	9,488,114	0
Family	6,404,890	11,322,047
Totals	21,941,646	32,529,959

Figure D-4: Total Gifting for Drake Family

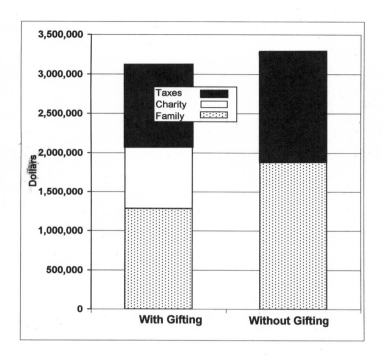

Chart - Lifetime Giving		
	With Gifting	Without Gifting
Taxes	1,026,614	1,387,499
Charity	803,009	0
Family	1,276,551	1,881,781
Totals	3,106,174	3,269,280

Figure D-5: Total Gifting for Emory Family

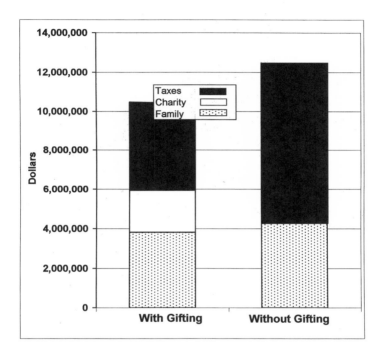

Chart - Lifetime Giving		
	With Gifting	Without Gifting
Taxes	4,515,499	8,178,026
Charity	2,124,621	0
Family	3,808,550	4,289,885
Totals	10,448,669	12,467,911

Figure D-6: Total Gifting for Finch Family

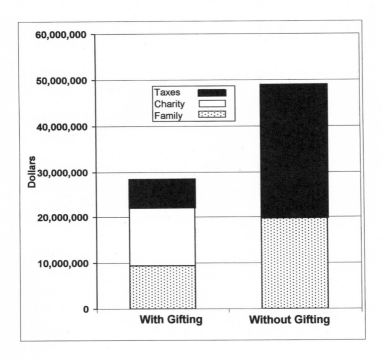

Chart - Lifetime Giving		
	With Gifting	Without Gifting
Taxes	6,090,787	28,909,872
Charity	12,968,575	0
Family	9,379,574	19,929,258
Totals	**28,438,935**	**48,839,130**

Appendix E
Detail Summary
and Hightlights

Table E-1: Total Gifting for Allen Family— Detail Summary

	With Gifting		Without Gifting		Difference
	Amount	%	Amount	%	
Taxes					
Income Taxes					
Ret'ment Plans	377,698		592,691		214,993
Other	645,590		808,650		163,060
Income Taxes - Total	1,023,288		1,401,342		378,053
Capital Gains Taxes	253,798		372,227		118,429
Estate Taxes	82,150		1,452,938		1,370,788
Total Taxes	1,359,237	31.6%	3,226,506	53.3%	1,867,270
Charity					
Annual	347,849		0		-347,849
At Death	337,762 *		0		-337,762
Total Charity	685,611	16.0%	0	0.0%	-685,611
Family					
Annual	347,849		0		-347,849
At Death	1,902,184		2,831,973 AY443		929,789
Total Family	2,250,033	52.4%	2,831,973	46.7%	581,940
Total Gifting	4,294,880	100.0%	6,058,479	100.0%	1,763,599

* From undistributed retirement plans.

Total Gifting for The Allen Family - Highlights

With Gifting, the Allen Family's				
Estate is reduced by:			1,937,941	
Income taxes are reduced by			378,053	
Capital Gains taxes are reduced by			118,429	
Estate taxes are reduced by			1,370,788	
Total taxes are reduced by			1,867,270	
Charities receive an average of	11,595	per year, or	347,849	during Allen's lifetime, plus
			337,762	at their death
	for a total lifetime charity gifting of		685,611	
Family receives an average of	11,595	per year, or	347,849	during Allen's lifetime, plus
			1,902,184	at their death
	for a total lifetime family gifting of		2,250,033	
In Addition:				
If the family members invest their annual gifting of			347,849	as they get it each year,
		it will grow to	1,132,187	
	and this, added to the		1,902,184	given at their death
	will add up to a total lifetime family gifting of		3,034,371	
		which compares with the	2,831,973	given at their death
that they would have received with the "without giving" scenario.				

191

Table E-2: Total Gifting for Brown Family—
Detail Summary

	With Gifting		Without Gifting		Difference
	Amount	%	Amount	%	
Taxes					
Income Taxes					
Ret'ment Plans	1,169,736		1,492,078		322,341
Other	595,965		1,387,328		791,363
Income Taxes - Total	1,765,701		2,879,406		1,113,704
Capital Gains Taxes	354,640		803,000		448,360
Estate Taxes	627,447		4,979,972		4,352,525
Total Taxes	2,747,788	28.4%	8,662,377	61.5%	5,914,589
Charity					
Annual	1,570,378		0		-1,570,378
At Death	1,813,087 *		0		-1,813,087
Total Charity	3,383,465	35.0%	0	0.0%	-3,383,465
Family					
Annual	1,121,699		0		-1,121,699
At Death	2,423,911		5,413,303 *AY443*		2,989,392
Total Family	3,545,610	36.6%	5,413,303	38.5%	1,867,693
Total Gifting	9,676,863	100.0%	14,075,681	100.0%	4,398,817

* From undistributed retirement plans.

Total Gifting for The Brown Family - Highlights

With Gifting, the Brown Family's				
Estate is reduced by:			5,599,238	
Income taxes are reduced by			1,113,704	
Capital Gains taxes are reduced by			448,360	
Estate taxes are reduced by			4,352,525	
Total taxes are reduced by			5,914,589	
Charities receive an average of	52,346	per year, or	1,570,378	during Brown's lifetime, plus
			1,813,087	at their death
	for a total lifetime charity gifting of		3,383,465	
Family receives an average of	37,390	per year, or	1,121,699	during Brown's lifetime, plus
			2,423,911	at their death
	for a total lifetime family gifting of		3,545,610	
In Addition:				
If the family members invest their annual gifting of			1,121,699	as they get it each year,
	it will grow to		3,155,480	
	and this, added to the		2,423,911	given at their death
will add up to a total lifetime family gifting of			5,579,392	
	which compares with the		5,413,303	given at their death
that they would have received with the "without giving" scenario.				

Table E-3: Total Gifting for Clark Family— Detail Summary

	With Gifting		Without Gifting		Difference
	Amount	%	Amount	%	
Taxes					
Income Taxes					
Ret'ment Plans	3,197,309		3,197,309		0
Other	700,225		3,215,040		2,514,816
Income Taxes - Total	3,897,534		6,412,349		2,514,816
Capital Gains Taxes	770,917		1,956,667		1,185,750
Estate Taxes	1,380,192		12,838,897		11,458,704
Total Taxes	6,048,643	27.6%	21,207,912	65.2%	15,159,270
Charity					
Annual	3,925,946		0		-3,925,946
At Death	5,562,168 *		0		-5,562,168
Total Charity	9,488,114	43.2%	0	0.0%	-9,488,114
Family					
Annual	3,365,096		0		-3,365,096
At Death	3,039,794		11,322,047 *AY443*		8,282,253
Total Family	6,404,890	29.2%	11,322,047	34.8%	4,917,157
Total Gifting	21,941,646	100.0%	32,529,959	100.0%	10,588,313

* From undistributed retirement plans.

Total Gifting for The Clark Family - Highlights

With Gifting, the Clark Family's				
Estate is reduced by:			14,502,397	
Income taxes are reduced by			2,514,816	
Capital Gains taxes are reduced by			1,185,750	
Estate taxes are reduced by			11,458,704	
Total taxes are reduced by			15,159,270	
Charities receive an average of	130,865	per year, or	3,925,946	during Clark's lifetime, plus
			5,562,168	at their death
	for a total lifetime charity gifting of		9,488,114	
Family receives an average of	112,170	per year, or	3,365,096	during Clark's lifetime, plus
			3,039,794	at their death
	for a total lifetime family gifting of		6,404,890	
In Addition:				
If the family members invest their annual gifting of			3,365,096	as they get it each year,
		it will grow to	9,457,703	
	and this, added to the		3,039,794	given at their death
	will add up to a total lifetime family gifting of		12,497,496	
	which compares with the		11,322,047	given at their death
that they would have received with the "without giving" scenario.				

Table E-4: Total Gifting for Drake Family— Detail Summary

	With Gifting		Without Gifting		Difference
	Amount	%	Amount	%	
Taxes					
Income Taxes					
Ret'ment Plans	308,620		331,143		22,522
Other	600,620		671,709		71,089
Income Taxes - Total	909,241		1,002,852		93,611
Capital Gains Taxes	117,373		132,143		14,770
Estate Taxes	0		252,505		252,505
Total Taxes	1,026,614	33.1%	1,387,499	42.4%	360,886
Charity					
Annual	132,878		0		-132,878
At Death	670,132 *		0		-670,132
Total Charity	803,009	25.9%	0	0.0%	-803,009
Family					
Annual	132,878		0		-132,878
At Death	1,143,674		1,881,781 AY443		738,107
Total Family	1,276,551	41.1%	1,881,781	57.6%	605,229
Total Gifting	3,106,174	100.0%	3,269,280	100.0%	163,106

* From undistributed retirement plans.

Total Gifting for The Drake Family - Highlights

With Gifting, the Drake Family's				
Estate is reduced by:			372,641	
Income taxes are reduced by			93,611	
Capital Gains taxes are reduced by			14,770	
Estate taxes are reduced by			252,505	
Total taxes are reduced by			360,886	
Charities receive an average of	4,429	per year, or	132,878	during Drake's lifetime, plus
			670,132	at their death
	for a total lifetime charity gifting of		803,009	
Family receives an average of	4,429	per year, or	132,878	during Drake's lifetime, plus
			1,143,674	at their death
	for a total lifetime family gifting of		1,276,551	
In Addition:				
If the family members invest their annual gifting of			132,878	as they get it each year,
		it will grow to	139,017	
	and this, added to the		1,143,674	given at their death
	will add up to a total lifetime family gifting of		1,282,690	
	which compares with the		1,881,781	given at their death
that they would have received with the "without giving" scenario.				

Table E-5: Total Gifting for Emory Family— Detail Summary

	With Gifting		Without Gifting		Difference
	Amount	%	Amount	%	
Taxes					
Income Taxes					
Ret'ment Plans	1,327,953		1,327,953		0
Other	1,951,040		3,074,526		1,123,486
Income Taxes - Total	3,278,993		4,402,479		1,123,486
Capital Gains Taxes	630,430		860,110		229,680
Estate Taxes	606,076		2,915,438		2,309,361
Total Taxes	4,515,499	43.2%	8,178,026	65.6%	3,662,527
Charity					
Annual	1,289,954		0		-1,289,954
At Death	834,667 *		0		-834,667
Total Charity	2,124,621	20.3%	0	0.0%	-2,124,621
Family					
Annual	1,402,123		0		-1,402,123
At Death	2,406,426		4,289,885 AY443		1,883,459
Total Family	3,808,550	36.5%	4,289,885	34.4%	481,335
Total Gifting	10,448,669	100.0%	12,467,911	100.0%	2,019,242

* From undistributed retirement plans.

Total Gifting for The Emory Family - Highlights

With Gifting, the Emory Family's				
Estate is reduced by:			3,217,320	
Income taxes are reduced by			1,123,486	
Capital Gains taxes are reduced by			229,680	
Estate taxes are reduced by			2,309,361	
Total taxes are reduced by			3,662,527	
Charities receive an average of	42,998	per year, or	1,289,954	during Emory's lifetime, plus
			834,667	at their death
	for a total lifetime charity gifting of		2,124,621	
Family receives an average of	46,737	per year, or	1,402,123	during Emory's lifetime, plus
			2,406,426	at their death
	for a total lifetime family gifting of		3,808,550	
In Addition:				
If the family members invest their annual gifting of			1,402,123	as they get it each year,
	it will grow to		1,458,489	
	and this, added to the		2,406,426	given at their death
	will add up to a total lifetime family gifting of		3,864,915	
	which compares with the		4,289,885	given at their death
that they would have received with the "without giving" scenario.				

Table E-6: Total Gifting for Finch Family— Detail Summary

	With Gifting		Without Gifting		Difference
	Amount	%	Amount	%	
Taxes					
Income Taxes					
Ret'ment Plans	34,041		45,769		11,728
Other	522,969		3,517,417		2,994,448
Income Taxes - Total	557,010		3,563,186		3,006,176
Capital Gains Taxes	2,159,157		3,026,710		867,553
Estate Taxes	3,374,619		22,319,975		18,945,356
Total Taxes	6,090,787	21.4%	28,909,872	59.2%	22,819,085
Charity					
Annual	12,582,575		0		-12,582,575
At Death	386,000 *		0		-386,000
Total Charity	12,968,575	45.6%	0	0.0%	-12,968,575
Family					
Annual	4,707,977		0		-4,707,977
At Death	4,671,598		19,929,258 AY443		15,257,661
Total Family	9,379,574	33.0%	19,929,258	40.8%	10,549,684
Total Gifting	28,438,935	100.0%	48,839,130	100.0%	20,400,195

* From undistributed retirement plans.

Total Gifting for The Finch Family - Highlights

With Gifting, the Finch Family's			
Estate is reduced by:		33,838,759	
Income taxes are reduced by		3,006,176	
Capital Gains taxes are reduced by		867,553	
Estate taxes are reduced by		18,945,356	
Total taxes are reduced by		22,819,085	
Charities receive an average of	419,419	per year, or	12,582,575	during Finch's lifetime, plus
			386,000	at their death
	for a total lifetime charity gifting of		12,968,575	
Family receives an average of	156,933	per year, or	4,707,977	during Finch's lifetime, plus
			4,671,598	at their death
	for a total lifetime family gifting of		9,379,574	
In Addition:				
If the family members invest their annual gifting of		4,707,977	as they get it each year,
	it will grow to	14,402,962	
	and this, added to the	4,671,598	given at their death
	will add up to a total lifetime family gifting of	19,074,560	
	which compares with the	19,929,258	given at their death
	that they would have received with the "without giving" scenario.		